Higgs Boson

Edited By
Harun Selvitopi

Higgs Boson: A Mathematical Survey with Finite Element Method

Copyright © 2023 by Nova Science Publishers, Inc.

All rights reserved. No part of this book may be reproduced, stored in a retrieval system or transmitted in any form or by any means: electronic, electrostatic, magnetic, tape, mechanical photocopying, recording or otherwise without the written permission of the Publisher.

We have partnered with Copyright Clearance Center to make it easy for you to obtain permissions to reuse content from this publication. You can visit copyright.com and search by Title, ISBN, or ISSN.

For further questions about using the service on copyright.com, please contact:

Copyright Clearance Center
Phone: +1-(978) 750-8400 Fax: +1-(978) 750-4470 E-mail: info@copyright.com

NOTICE TO THE READER

The Publisher has taken reasonable care in the preparation of this book, but makes no expressed or implied warranty of any kind and assumes no responsibility for any errors or omissions. No liability is assumed for incidental or consequential damages in connection with or arising out of information contained in this book. The Publisher shall not be liable for any special, consequential, or exemplary damages resulting, in whole or in part, from the readers' use of, or reliance upon, this material. Any parts of this book based on government reports are so indicated and copyright is claimed for those parts to the extent applicable to compilations of such works.

Independent verification should be sought for any data, advice or recommendations contained in this book. In addition, no responsibility is assumed by the Publisher for any injury and/or damage to persons or property arising from any methods, products, instructions, ideas or otherwise contained in this publication.

This publication is designed to provide accurate and authoritative information with regards to the subject matter covered herein. It is sold with the clear understanding that the Publisher is not engaged in rendering legal or any other professional services. If legal or any other expert assistance is required, the services of a competent person should be sought. FROM A DECLARATION OF PARTICIPANTS JOINTLY ADOPTED BY A COMMITTEE OF THE AMERICAN BAR ASSOCIATION AND A COMMITTEE OF PUBLISHERS.

Library of Congress Cataloging-in-Publication Data

ISBN: 979-8-88697-785-1

Published by Nova Science Publishers, Inc. † New York

To my family

Contents

Preface ix

Introduction xi

1 Finite Difference Method for the Solution of Partial Differential Equations (PDE) 1
   1.1   FDM for Elliptic Equations 1
   1.2   FDM for Parabolic Equations 5
        1.2.1   Forward-Difference Method 5
        1.2.2   Backward-Difference Method 7
        1.2.3   Crank-Nicolson Method 9
        1.2.4   Stability Analysis of Finite Difference Method 11
        1.2.5   Exercises 15
   1.3   FDM for Hyperbolic Partial Differential Equations 18
        1.3.1   Stability Analysis 23

2 Finite Element Method for the Solution of Partial Differential Equations (PDE) 27
   2.1   The Development of the Finite Element Method 27
   2.2   Application of Finite Element Method to Partial Differential Equations 29
        2.2.1   Discretization 29
        2.2.2   Elements 29
        2.2.3   2-D Elements 30
        2.2.4   Shape Functions 31
        2.2.5   Triangular Elements Shape Functions 31
        2.2.6   Finite Element Method Formulation for Laplace Equation 32
        2.2.7   Weak Form for Laplace Equation 32
        2.2.8   Variational Form for Laplace Equation 34

3 The Numerical Integration Methods 37
   3.1   Newton-Type Integration Methods 37
        3.1.1   Trapezium Rule 37
        3.1.2   Simpson Method 38
   3.2   Gauss-Type Integration Methods 38
        3.2.1   Gauss-Legendre Method 38
   3.3   Two-Dimensional Numerical Integration 39

4 Finite Element Method Solution of Laplace Equation 43

Contents

5 One-Dimensional Wave Equation 45
   5.1   Finite Element Solution of One-Dimensional Wave Equation 45
   5.2   Central Difference Approximation 45

6 Finite Element Simulation of the One- and Two-Dimensional Wave Equation in Einstein and de Sitter Space-Time 47
   6.1   Application of the Numerical Method for One-Dimensional Problem 47
   6.2   Application of the Numerical Method for Two-Dimensional Problem 49

7 Root Finding Approximations 53
   7.1   Newton's Method 53
       7.1.1   Application of Newton Method 55
   7.2   Secant Method 55

8 Newton's Method for Nonlinear System of Equations in n−Dimension 59
   8.1   Newton Method 59
   8.2   Quasi-Newton Method 65
   8.3   Broyden Method 65

9 Finite Difference/Galerkin Finite Element Simulation of the Semi-Linear Wave Equation with Scale-Invariant Damping, Mass and Power Nonlinearity 69
   9.1   Application of the GFEM 70
   9.2   Application of the FDM 71
   9.3   Application of Newton Method 72

10 Higgs Boson in de Sitter Space-Time 73
   10.1 Mathematical Model of the Higgs Boson in de Sitter Space-Time 73
   10.2 Finite Element Method for Higgs Boson Equation 74
      10.2.1 Newton Method 76
   10.3 Numerical Results 77

References 81

Index 83

Preface

The finite element method (FEM) is a powerful numerical technique that can be used to solve partial differential equations (PDEs) that describe a wide range of physical phenomena. In the context of the Higgs boson, the FEM can be used to solve the PDEs that describe the Higgs boson, which is responsible for giving masses to other particles in the Standard Model of particle physics. In a de Sitter space-time, the Higgs boson would be affected by the expansion of the universe. This would introduce additional complexity to the PDEs that describe the Higgs boson, making use of the FEM to solve them even more challenging. De Sitter space-time is a solution of Einstein's equation with a positive cosmological constant which describes a universe with positive curvature and acceleration. To use the FEM to solve the Higgs boson equations in a de Sitter space-time, one would need to have a deep understanding of both the Higgs boson and the de Sitter space-time. This would likely require expertise in both particle physics and general relativity. The Higgs boson equations would need to be modified to account for the expansion of the universe, and the FEM solution would need to be adapted to take this into account. But it could offer a new perspective on the behavior of the Higgs boson in the early universe and could be a valuable area of research.

In addition to requiring a deep understanding of both the Higgs boson and de Sitter space-time, using the FEM to solve the Higgs boson equations in de Sitter space-time would also require significant computational resources and expertise. The FEM involves discretizing the continuous domain into a large number of small elements and solving the PDEs locally on each element. This can lead to a large number of unknowns and equations to solve, making it a computationally intensive task. Another challenge that must be taken into account when solving the Higgs boson equations in a de Sitter space-time using the FEM is dealing with the boundary conditions. The expansion of the universe would lead to different boundary conditions than in flat space-time, and these boundary conditions would need to be incorporated into the FEM solution. Additionally, the Higgs boson equation is a nonlinear equation, which makes it even more challenging to solve. Nonlinear equations often have multiple solutions, and the FEM solution would need to be able to identify the correct solution among these multiple solutions. Using the FEM to solve the Higgs boson equations in a de Sitter space-time is a challenging task that would require a deep understanding of both the Higgs boson and de Sitter space-time, significant computational resources and expertise, and the ability to deal with nonlinearity and boundary conditions. However, it could lead to new insights into the behavior of the Higgs boson in the early universe and could be a valuable area of research.

It is a challenging task that would require significant resources, expertise and a deep understanding of both particle physics and general relativity. However, solving the Higgs boson equations in a de Sitter space-time could offer new insights into the behavior of the Higgs boson in the early universe and could potentially have implications for our understanding of the universe's evolution and the nature of dark energy. Additionally, the study of Higgs boson in de Sitter space-time could shed light on the Higgs mechanism in the context of inflationary cosmology and the generation of primordial fluctuations. It could also have implications on the study of Higgs boson in the context of other alternative theories of gravity like scalar-tensor theories, theories with non-minimal couplings, etc. In order to achieve this, one would likely need to develop new numerical techniques and algorithms that are specifically designed to handle the complexities of solving PDEs in a de Sitter space-time. This would be a challenging and highly technical task, but it could lead to new discoveries and insights about the universe and fundamental physics.

Introduction

As it is known, one of the main research subjects of particle physics is the existence and experimental observation of the Higgs boson, which is thought to give matter its mass. The simulation of the Higgs boson, which was observed for a short time in 2012 as a result of the experiments carried out at CERN (European Nuclear Research Center) since its establishment in 1954, will also be a guide for scientists. The de Sitter metric describes the exponential expansion of the universe. In order to better observe the motion of matter, the mathematical model of the Higgs boson equation in de Sitter space-time has been put forward (Yagdjian et al., 2009). Then, it was focused on investigating the existence of the solution of the existing mathematical model. Yagdjian (2012), using Lp-Lq inequalities, proved the existence of the general solution of the Higgs boson equation in de Sitter space-time. In the same year, necessary conditions were given for the general solution of the aforementioned equation, and it was revealed that the solution to be obtained changed sign and oscillated as time progressed (Yagdjian, 2012). Using the energy inequality, the existence of the general solution of the Higgs boson equation in Sitter space-time has been shown (Nakamura, 2014). (Yagdjian et al., 2018) demonstrated the maximum principle of the Higgs boson equation in de Sitter space-time and visualized the change of bubbles over time. With the above-mentioned theoretical studies, the existence of the general solution of the Higgs boson equation in de Sitter space-time has been revealed and information about how the general solution will move in time is presented. Moreover, the necessary conditions for obtaining the general solution have been put forward. The analytical (real) solution of the aforementioned equation could not be obtained. Therefore, they have focused on to obtain the numerical solution. In this context (Balogh et al., 2019), the numerical solution using the fourth-order advanced Runge-Kutta scheme in time discretization and the fourth-order finite difference discretization in space has been obtained for the 3+1 dimensional Higgs Boson equation in de Sitter space-time. As it is known, the finite difference method is basically derived from the Taylor series expansion. While this method is being introduced, a significant number of terms of the Taylor series are truncated, resulting in a truncation error arising from the method. However, it is easier to apply to problems compared to numerical methods, which have certain advantages in other literature. In the finite element method, since the elements of the obtained element matrices are based on the integral calculation over the elements in the network, it is clear that the error to be caused by the numerical solution to be obtained by the finite element method will be less than the error to be obtained by the finite difference method.

Floating Point

Computer numbers (floating point numbers) are used in the calculation phase while obtaining numerical solutions. Generally used computer numbers are chosen with single or double precision. Since the spatial dimension of the problem we are considering is 3 and nonlinear type, quad-precision computer numbers will be used rather than single- and double-precision computer numbers. In this way, it is thought that the error caused by rounding the computer numbers will be minimized and solutions closer to the real solution will be obtained.

Chapter 1

Finite Difference Method for the Solution of Partial Differential Equations (PDE)

We can consider the

$$k\phi_{xx} + l\phi_{xy} + m\phi_{yy} = f, \tag{1.1}$$

where k, l and m are the functions of x, y, ϕ, ϕ_x and ϕ_y. We can define the discriminant as:

$$l^2 - 4km.$$

We can determine the type of (1.1) with respect to discriminant:

- $l^2 - 4km < 0$ then the partial differential equation is elliptic type.
- $l^2 - 4km = 0$ then the partial differential equation is parabolic type.
- $l^2 - 4km > 0$ then the partial differential equation is hyperbolic type.

After categorizing the PDEs, we will solve them numerically because obtaining the analytical solution of most of the PDEs is very difficult.

1.1. FDM for Elliptic Equations

The common elliptic partial differential equations involve $\phi_{xx} + \phi_{yy}$ term. If the equation is the form

$$\phi_{xx} + \phi_{yy} = f(x, y)$$

then it is called Poisson's equation. If $f(x, y) = 0$, then we call the PDE Laplace equation.

It is known that the exact solution of PDE is to satisfy the equation in the problem domain and the boundary of the domain. In the finite difference method, we are aiming to obtain the approximation solution of the PDE at the grid(mesh) points. For this purpose, we consider the derivative approximations using Taylor series expansion. The Taylor series expansion in two-dimensional (2–D) for the variables x and y are like below:

$$\phi(x + \delta x, y) = \phi(x, y) + \delta x \phi_x(x, y) + \frac{\delta x^2}{2} \phi_{xx}(x, y) + \cdots \tag{1.2}$$

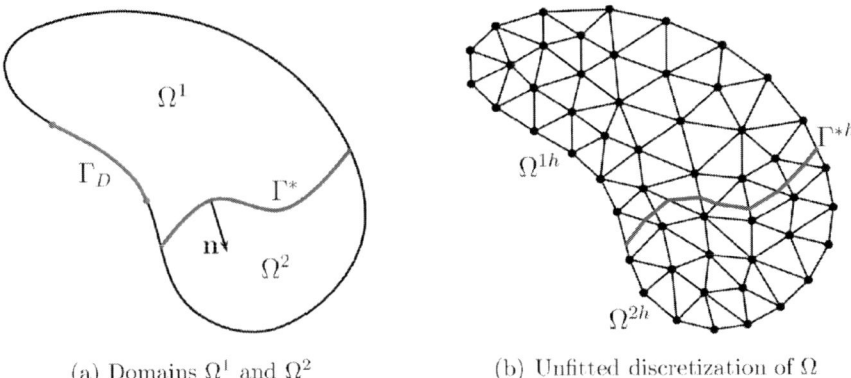

(a) Domains Ω^1 and Ω^2 (b) Unfitted discretization of Ω

Figure 1.1. Domain discretization

$$\phi(x, y + \delta y) = \phi(x, y) + \delta y \phi_y(x, y) + \frac{\delta y^2}{2} \phi_{yy}(x, y) + \cdots \quad (1.3)$$

$$\phi(x - \delta x, y) = \phi(x, y) - \delta x \phi_x(x, y) + \frac{\delta x^2}{2} \phi_{xx}(x, y) + \cdots \quad (1.4)$$

$$\phi(x, y - \delta y) = \phi(x, y) - \delta y \phi_y(x, y) + \frac{\delta y^2}{2} \phi_{yy}(x, y) + \cdots \quad (1.5)$$

using (1.2), we obtain the:
$$\phi_x = \frac{\phi(x + \delta x, y) - \phi(x, y)}{\delta x},$$

forward difference approximation for $\phi_x(x, y)$.

Using (1.4), we obtain the:
$$\phi_x = \frac{\phi(x, y) - \phi(x - \delta x, y)}{\delta x},$$

backward difference approximation for $\phi_x(x, y)$.

Then we consider (1.2)-(1.4),
$$\phi_x = \frac{\phi(x + \delta x, y) - \phi(x - \delta x, y)}{2\delta x},$$

and obtain the central difference approximation (CDA) for $\phi_x(x, y)$.

With a similar thought, using (1.3),
$$\phi_y = \frac{\phi(x, y + \delta y) - \phi(x, y)}{\delta y},$$

we obtain the forward difference approximation for $\phi_y(x, y)$.

Then taking into account (1.5),
$$\phi_y = \frac{\phi(x, y) - \phi(x, y - \delta y)}{\delta y},$$

we obtain the backward difference approximation for $\phi_y(x, y)$.

Finally, considering (1.3)–(1.5),

$$\phi_y = \frac{\phi(x, y + \delta y) - \phi(x, y - \delta y)}{2\delta y},$$

we obtain the central difference approximation for $\phi_y(x, y)$.

We can also obtain the second-order partial derivatives of the unknown function with respect to variables. Therefore we consider (1.2)–(1.4),

$$\phi_{xx} = \frac{\phi(x + \delta x, y) - 2\phi(x, y) + \phi(x - \delta x, y)}{\delta x^2},$$

and obtain the central difference approximation for $\phi_{xx}(x, y)$.

Similarly, using (1.3)–(1.5),

$$\phi_{yy} = \frac{\phi(x, y + \delta y) - 2\phi(x, y) + \phi(x, y - \delta y)}{\delta y^2},$$

we obtain the central difference approximation for $\phi_{yy}(x, y)$.

In the approximate solution procedure, the error occurs between the exact and approximate solution, and the types of errors are the following.

1. Truncation Error
   We can observe the Laplace equation $\phi_{xx}(x, y) + \phi_{yy}(x, y) = 0$. The truncation error of the Laplace equation occurs when we approximate with the finite difference method: $O(\delta x^2) + O(\delta y^2)$, where O is the big-O notation.
2. Round-off Error
   It occurs in the finite difference method due to the nature of the Taylor series expansion. It can be reduced using workstations (supercomputers), considering the double precision or quadra precision operations.
3. Discretization Error
   This type of error occurs on account of the Discretization of the solution domain.

Example 1.1.1 *Obtain the finite difference solution of the 2−D Laplace equation on a square domain. For example $\phi xx(x, y) + \phi yy(x, y) = 0$ on a square domain $0 \leq x \leq 1$, $0 \leq y \leq 1$ with the boundary conditions $\phi(x, 0) = h_1(x)$, $\phi(x, 1) = h_2(x)$, $\phi(0, y) = k_1(x)$ and $\phi(1, y) = k_2(x)$.*

Solution 1. We discretize the Laplace equation with finite difference approximation,

$$\frac{\phi_{i+1,j} - 2\phi_{i,j} + \phi_{i-1,j}}{\delta x^2} + \frac{\phi_{i,j+1} - 2\phi_{i,j} + \phi_{i,j-1}}{\delta y^2} = 0 \tag{1.6}$$

then simplifying the equation, we will get

$$\frac{1}{\delta y^2}\phi_{i,j+1} + \frac{1}{\delta x^2}\phi_{i+1,j} - 2\frac{1}{\delta x^2 + \delta y^2}\phi_{i,j} + \frac{1}{\delta x^2}\phi_{i-1,j} + \frac{1}{\delta y^2}\phi_{i,j-1} = 0 \tag{1.7}$$

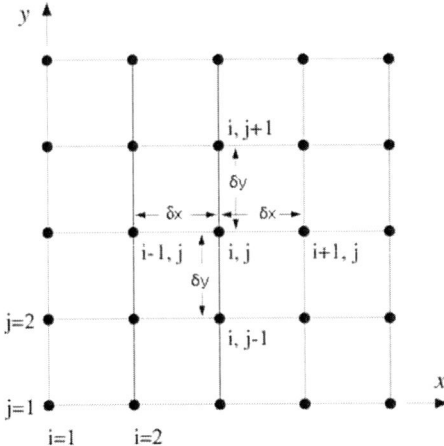

Figure 1.2. Discretization of the solution domain

then we obtain the matrix-vector form of the system of equations as:

$$\begin{bmatrix} -2\frac{1}{\delta x^2 + \delta y^2} & \frac{1}{\delta x^2} & 0 & \vdots & \frac{1}{\delta y^2} & 0 & \vdots & \ddots \\ \frac{1}{\delta x^2} & -2\frac{1}{\delta x^2 + \delta y^2} & \frac{1}{\delta x^2} & 0 & \cdots & \frac{1}{\delta y^2} & 0 & \cdots & \ddots \\ \ddots & \ddots & 0 & \cdots & \ddots & 0 & \cdots & \ddots \\ \frac{1}{\delta y^2} & 0 & \frac{1}{\delta x^2} & -2\frac{1}{\delta x^2+\delta y^2} & \frac{1}{\delta x^2} & 0 & \cdots & \frac{1}{\delta y^2} & 0 & \cdots \\ 0 & \frac{1}{\delta y^2} & 0 & \frac{1}{\delta x^2} & -2\frac{1}{\delta x^2+\delta y^2} & \frac{1}{\delta x^2} & \cdots & 0 & \frac{1}{\delta y^2} & \cdots \\ \ddots & \ddots & 0 & \cdots & \ddots & 0 & \cdots & \ddots \end{bmatrix} \begin{bmatrix} \phi_{11} \\ \vdots \\ \phi_{n1} \\ \phi_{12} \\ \vdots \\ \phi_{n2} \\ \vdots \\ \phi_{1m} \\ \vdots \\ \phi_{nm} \end{bmatrix} = \begin{bmatrix} 0 \\ 0 \\ \vdots \\ 0 \end{bmatrix},$$

and then apply the boundary condition and solve the matrix-vector system to obtain the finite difference solution of the Laplace equation.

Exercise 1. Solve the elliptic partial differential equation using finite difference method $\frac{\partial^2 \phi}{\partial x^2} + \frac{\partial^2 \phi}{\partial x^2} = 0$, $0 \leq x \leq 1$ $0 \leq y \leq 1$ with $u(x,0) = 2x$, $u(x,1) = x^2$ $u(1,y) = \ln(y)$, $u(0,y) = \ln(y^2 + 3)$.

Exercise 2. Solve the Poisson's equation using finite difference method $\frac{\partial^2 \phi}{\partial x^2} + \frac{\partial^2 \phi}{\partial x^2} = 2$, $0 \leq x \leq 2$ $0 \leq y \leq 2$ with $u(x,0) = x^2+1$, $u(x,2) = x^2$ $u(0,y) = y^2$, $u(2,y) = (y-2)^2$.

Exercise 3. Obtain the approximate solution of the elliptic equation using finite difference method $\frac{\partial^2 \phi}{\partial x^2} + \frac{\partial^2 \phi}{\partial x^2} = 0$, $0 \leq x \leq 1$ $0 \leq y \leq 1$ with $u(x,0) = x$, $u(x,1) = 0$ $u(0,y) = y$, $u(1,y) = 0$.

Exercise 4. Solve the Poisson's equation using finite difference method $\frac{\partial^2 \phi}{\partial x^2} + \frac{\partial^2 \phi}{\partial x^2} = cos(x+y) + cos(x-y)$, $0 \leq x \leq \pi$ $0 \leq y \leq \pi/2$ with $u(x,0) = -cos(x)$, $u(x,\pi/2) = 0$ $u(0,y) = -cos(y)$, $u(\pi,y) = cos(y)$.

Exercise 5. Solve the Poisson's equation using finite difference method $\frac{\partial^2 \phi}{\partial x^2} + \frac{\partial^2 \phi}{\partial x^2} = \frac{x}{y} + \frac{y}{x}$, $1 \leq x \leq 2$ $0 \leq y \leq 2$ with $u(x,1) = ln(x)$, $u(x,2) = ln(x^2)$ $u(0,y) = ln(y)$, $u(2,y) = yln(y)$.

1.2. FDM for Parabolic Equations

We consider the heat equation as a parabolic partial differential equation in one-dimensional form (1−D):

$$\frac{\partial \phi}{\partial t} = a^2 \frac{\partial^2 \phi}{\partial x^2} \quad 0 < x < l, \quad t > 0 \tag{1.8}$$

with the initial and boundary conditions

$$\phi(0,t) = \phi(l,t) = g(x) \quad t > 0, \quad \phi(x,0) = f(x), \quad 0 \leq x \leq l.$$

To obtain the approximate solution of the parabolic partial differential equation, we use the finite difference method. Firstly, we take an integer to determine the space step size and calculate $\delta x = (l-0)/m$. With the same perspective, we chose n integer to determine the time step size $\delta t = (t_{end} - t_{start})/n$. Then, we assign the grid points (x_i, t_j) where $x_i = \delta x i$ and $t_j = \delta t j$ for $i = 0, 1, \ldots m$ and $j = 0, 1, \ldots$

1.2.1 Forward-Difference Method

We discretize the time variable via the finite difference method using the Taylor series.

$$\frac{\partial \phi}{\partial t}(x_i, t_j) \approx \frac{\phi(x_i, t_j + \delta t) - \phi(x_i, t_j)}{\delta t} \tag{1.9}$$

for some (t_j, t_{j+1}), and we also discretize the spatial variable using finite difference method

$$\frac{\partial^2 \phi}{\partial x^2}(x_i, t_j) \approx \frac{\phi(x_i + \delta x, t_j) - 2\phi(x_i, t_j) + \phi(x_i - \delta x, t_j)}{\delta x^2} \tag{1.10}$$

for (x_{i-1}, x_{i+1}).
If we consider

$$\frac{\partial \phi}{\partial t} = a^2 \frac{\partial^2 \phi}{\partial x^2}, \tag{1.11}$$

then applying the difference quotients we obtain

$$\frac{\phi(x_i, t_j + \delta t) - \phi(x_i, t_j)}{\delta t} = a^2 \frac{\phi(x_i + \delta x, t_j) - 2\phi(x_i, t_j) + \phi(x_i - \delta x, t_j)}{\delta x^2}, \tag{1.12}$$

then we rewrite it,

$$\frac{\phi_{i,j+1} - \phi_{i,j}}{\delta t} = a^2 \frac{\phi_{i+1,j} - 2\phi_{i,j} + \phi_{i-1,j}}{\delta x^2}. \tag{1.13}$$

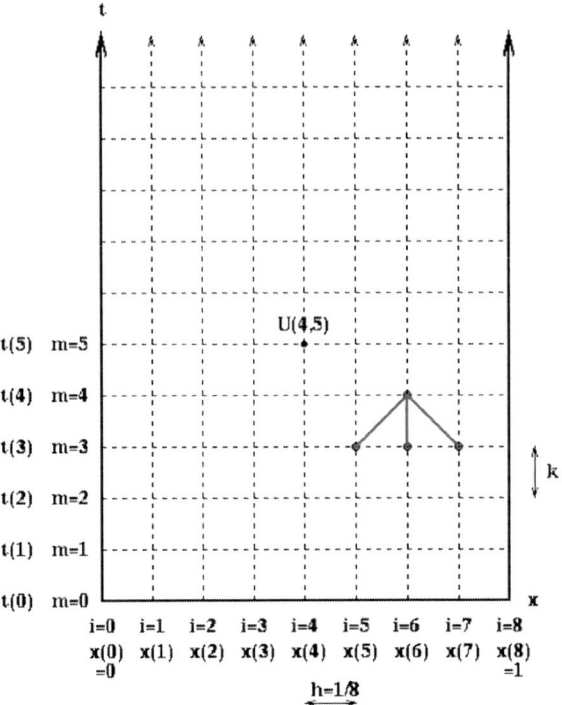

Figure 1.3. Discretization of 1D heat equation

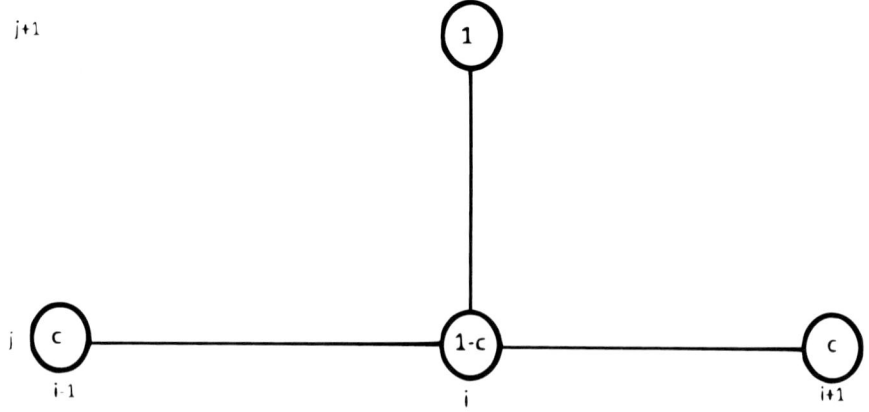

Figure 1.4. Computational molecule of 1D heat equation with explicit finite difference method

We know the values $\phi_{i,0}$ $i = 0, 1, \ldots, n+1$ from the initial condition, and we also know $\phi_{0,j}$ and $\phi_{n+1,j}$ $j = 0, 1, \ldots, m+1$. Therefore, the unknowns are $\phi_{i,j}$, $1 \leq i \leq n$ and $1 \leq j \leq m$. Under these conditions, we can write the explicit finite difference method for the 1D heat equation as:

$$\phi_{i,j+1} = \phi_{i,j} + \alpha^2 \frac{\delta t}{\delta x^2} \left(\phi_{i+,j} - 2\phi_{i,j} + \phi_{i-1,j} \right). \tag{1.14}$$

Table 1.1. The forward difference approximation results and exact solution of the heat equation

x_i	$\phi(x_i, 0.5)$	$k = 5.10^{-4}$	$|\phi(x_i, 0.5) - \phi_{i,1000}|$
0.0	0	0	0
0.1	0.222×10^{-5}	0.229×10^{-5}	6.411×10^{-5}
0.2	0.422×10^{-5}	0.434×10^{-5}	1.219×10^{-4}
0.3	0.581×10^{-5}	0.599×10^{-5}	1.678×10^{-4}
0.4	0.684×10^{-5}	0.700×10^{-5}	1.973×10^{-4}
0.5	0.720×10^{-5}	0.740×10^{-5}	2.075×10^{-4}
0.6	0.683×10^{-5}	0.703×10^{-5}	1.973×10^{-4}
0.7	0.581×10^{-5}	0.599×10^{-5}	1.678×10^{-4}
0.8	0.422×10^{-5}	0.435×10^{-5}	1.219×10^{-4}
0.9	0.222×10^{-5}	0.228×10^{-5}	6.511×10^{-5}
1.0	0	0	0

Example 1.2.1 *Solve the heat equation using forward difference approximation considering* $\delta t = 10^{-1}$, $\delta x = 5.10^{-4}$

$$\frac{\partial \phi}{\partial t} = \frac{\partial^2 \phi}{\partial x^2} \quad 0 < x < 1, \quad t > 0, \tag{1.15}$$

with boundary conditions

$$\phi(0, t) = \phi(1, t) = 0, \quad t > 0,$$

with the initial condition

$$\phi(x, 0) = \sin(\pi x), \quad 0 \leq x \leq 1.$$

Compare the numerical solution with the exact solution

$$\phi(x, t) = e^{-\pi^2 t} \sin(\pi x).$$

Solution 2. We apply the forward finite difference approximation for $c = a^2 \frac{\delta t}{\delta x^2} = (1)^2 (5.10^{-4}/10^{-1}) = 5.10^{-2}$ obtained from $\delta t = 10^{-1}$, $\delta x = 5.10^{-4}$ values. Table 1.1 shows the forward difference approximation results, exact solution and error between the forward finite difference approximation and exact solution of the considered heat equation at time 0.5.

1.2.2 Backward-Difference Method

The type of the method (forward, backward or Crank-Nicolson) depends on the approximation of the time derivative. Therefore we consider the time quotient $\left(\frac{\partial \phi}{\partial t}(x_i, t_j)\right)$ as:

$$\frac{\partial \phi}{\partial t}(x_i, t_j) \approx \frac{\phi(x_i, t_{j+1}) - \phi(x_i, t_j)}{\delta t}$$

and for the space quotient

$$\frac{\partial^2 \phi}{\partial x^2}(x_i, t_j) \approx \frac{\phi(x_i + \delta x, t_{j+1}) - 2\phi(x_i, t_{j+1}) + \phi(x_i - \delta x, t_{j+1})}{\delta x^2}.$$

We discretize the term ϕ_{xx} on time level $j+1$ and obtain

$$\frac{\phi(x_i, t_{j+1}) - \phi(x_i, t_j)}{\delta t} = \alpha^2 \frac{\phi(x_i + \delta x, t_{j+1}) - 2\phi(x_i, t_{j+1}) + \phi(x_i - \delta x, t_{j+1})}{\delta x^2} \quad (1.16)$$

for each $i = 1, 2, \ldots, m$ and $j = 1, 2, \ldots$

The backward method includes the grid points (x_i, t_{j-1}), (x_{i-1}, t_j) and (x_{i+1}, t_j) to obtain the (x_i, t_j) value.

The computational molecule of the backward (implicit) finite difference method for the 1−D heat equation as:

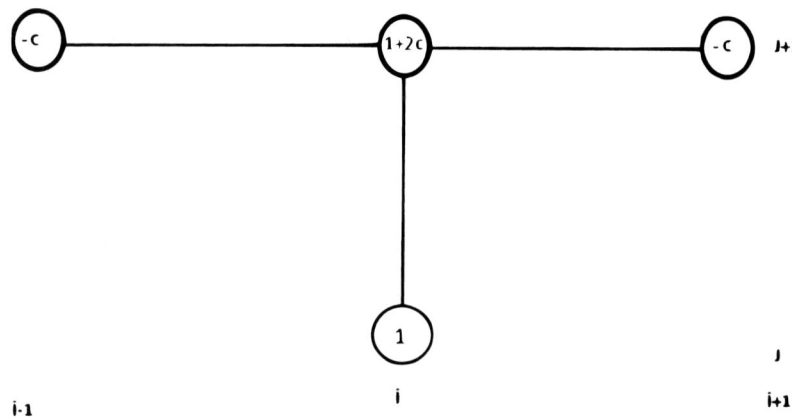

Figure 1.5. Computational molecule of 1D heat equation with implicit finite difference method

In the forward finite difference method, we can calculate the unknown $\phi_{i,j+1}$ using $\phi_{i-1,j}, \phi_{i,j}$ and $\phi_{i+1,j}$ points directly. As opposed to this, in the backward finite difference method, we cannot find the unknown point directly. Therefore, we solve the matrix-vector system of the equations (1.16) to find $\phi_{i,j+1}$.

Using the initial condition, we know $\phi_{i,j}$ and we also know the point which is on the boundary of the solution domain. Therefore, we get the matrix-vector system of linear equations,

$$\begin{bmatrix} 1+2c & -c & 0 & \ldots & 0 \\ -c & \ddots & \ddots & \ddots & \vdots \\ 0 & \ddots & \ddots & \ddots & 0 \\ \vdots & \ddots & \ddots & \ddots & -c \\ 0 & \ldots & 0 & -c & 1+2c \end{bmatrix} \begin{bmatrix} \phi_{1,j} \\ \phi_{2,j} \\ \vdots \\ \phi_{m-1,j} \end{bmatrix} = \begin{bmatrix} \phi_{1,j-1} \\ \phi_{2,j-1} \\ \vdots \\ \phi_{m-1,j-1} \end{bmatrix} \quad (1.17)$$

or $H\Phi^{j+1} = \Phi^j$ for each $i = 1, 2, \ldots$ This matrix-vector system is called three-band system. Thus, we have to know to solve a linear system to calculate Φ^{j+1} from Φ^j.

Table 1.2. The forward difference approximation results and exact solution of the heat equation

x_i	$\phi(x_i, 0.5)$	$k = 10^{-2}$	$|\phi(x_i, 0.5) - \phi_{i,50}|$
0.0	0	0	0
0.1	0.290×10^{-5}	0.222×10^{-5}	6.756×10^{-4}
0.2	0.551×10^{-5}	0.422×10^{-5}	1.285×10^{-3}
0.3	0.758×10^{-5}	0.581×10^{-5}	1.769×10^{-3}
0.4	0.891×10^{-5}	0.684×10^{-5}	2.079×10^{-3}
0.5	0.938×10^{-5}	0.719×10^{-5}	2.186×10^{-3}
0.6	0.891×10^{-5}	0.684×10^{-5}	2.079×10^{-3}
0.7	0.759×10^{-5}	0.581×10^{-5}	1.769×10^{-3}
0.8	0.551×10^{-5}	0.422×10^{-5}	1.285×10^{-3}
0.9	0.289×10^{-5}	0.222×10^{-5}	6.756×10^{-4}
1.0	0	0	0

Example 1.2.2 *Solve the heat equation using the backward finite difference method considering $\delta t = 10^{-1}$, $\delta x = 10^{-2}$*

$$\frac{\partial \phi}{\partial t} = \frac{\partial^2 \phi}{\partial x^2} \quad 0 < x < 1, \quad t > 0 \tag{1.18}$$

with boundary conditions

$$\phi(0, t) = \phi(1, t) = 0, \quad t > 0,$$

with the initial condition

$$\phi(x, 0) = sin(\pi x), \quad 0 \leq x \leq 1.$$

Compare the numerical solution with the exact solution

$$\phi(x, t) = e^{-\pi^2 t} sin(\pi x).$$

Solution 3. We apply the backward-difference method for $c = \alpha^2 \frac{\delta t}{\delta x^2} = (1)^2 (10^{-2}/10^{-1}) = 10^{-1}$ obtained from $\delta t = 10^{-1}$, $\delta x = 10^{-2}$ values. Table 8.1 shows the backward finite difference approximation results, exact solution and the error between the backward finite difference results and exact solution of the considered heat equation at time 0.5.

1.2.3 Crank-Nicolson Method

The Crank-Nicolson method is the average of the forward-difference method at *jth* time step in t and backward-difference method at $(j+1)st$ time step in t, for the space derivative term ϕ_{xx}. The local truncation error in the forward-difference method is

$$\varsigma_F = \frac{\delta t}{2} \frac{|\partial^2 \phi}{\partial t^2}(x_i, \gamma_j^1) + O(\delta^2),$$

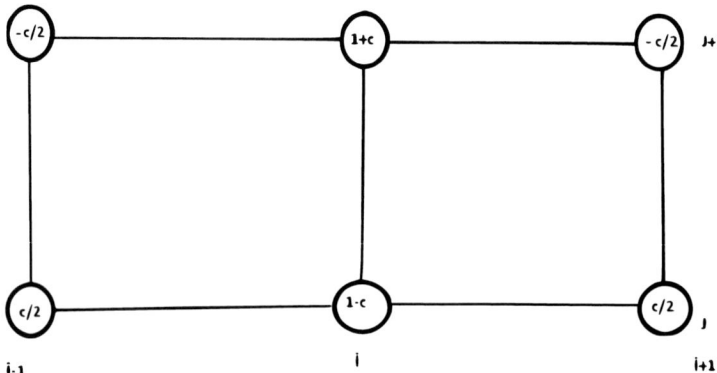

Figure 1.6. Computational molecule of 1D heat equation with Crank-Nicolson finite difference method

and the local truncation error in the backward-difference method is

$$\varsigma_B = -\frac{\delta t}{2} \frac{\partial^2 \phi}{\partial t^2}(x_i, \gamma_j^2) + O(\delta^2).$$

Then we choose

$$\frac{\partial^2 \phi}{\partial t^2}(x_i, \gamma_j^2) \approx \frac{\partial^2 \phi}{\partial t^2}(x_i, \gamma_j^1),$$

and we can formulate the Crank-Nicolson method as:

$$\frac{\phi_{i,j+1} - \phi_{i,j}}{\delta t} = \frac{\alpha^2}{2} \left[\frac{\phi_{i+1,j+1} - 2\phi_{i,j+1} + \phi_{i-1,j+1}}{\delta x^2} + \frac{\phi_{i+1,j} - 2\phi_{i,j} + \phi_{i-1,j}}{\delta x^2} \right] \quad (1.19)$$

with the local truncation error $O(\delta t^2 + \delta x^2)$.

We can write the system of linear equation in matrix-vector form as:

$$H\Phi^{j+1} = K\Phi^j \quad j = 1, 2, \ldots \quad (1.20)$$

where

$$H = \begin{bmatrix} 1+c & \frac{-c}{2} & 0 & \ldots & 0 \\ \frac{-c}{2} & \ddots & \ddots & \ddots & \vdots \\ 0 & \ddots & \ddots & \ddots & 0 \\ \vdots & \ddots & \ddots & \ddots & \frac{-c}{2} \\ 0 & \ldots & 0 & \frac{-c}{2} & 1+c \end{bmatrix}$$

and

$$K = \begin{bmatrix} 1-c & \frac{c}{2} & 0 & \ldots & 0 \\ \frac{c}{2} & \ddots & \ddots & \ddots & \vdots \\ 0 & \ddots & \ddots & \ddots & 0 \\ \vdots & \ddots & \ddots & \ddots & \frac{c}{2} \\ 0 & \ldots & 0 & \frac{c}{2} & 1-c \end{bmatrix}$$

Then we can generalize the approximations:

$$\phi_{xx} = \theta \phi_{,j+1} + (1-\theta)\phi_{,j}$$

where $\theta \in [0, 1]$,

- $\theta = 0 \rightarrow$ Explicit Method
- $\theta = \frac{1}{2} \rightarrow$ Crank-Nicolson Method
- $\theta = 1 \rightarrow$ Implicit Method

Example 1.2.3 *Solve the heat equation numerically using Crank-Nicolson method considering $\delta t = 10^{-1}$, $\delta x = 10^{-2}$*

$$\frac{\partial \phi}{\partial t} = \frac{\partial^2 \phi}{\partial x^2} \quad 0 < x < 1, \quad t > 0 \tag{1.21}$$

with boundary conditions

$$\phi(0, t) = \phi(1, t) = 0, \quad t > 0,$$

with the initial condition

$$\phi(x, 0) = \sin(\pi x), \quad 0 \leq x \leq 1.$$

Compare the numerical solution with the exact solution

$$\phi(x, t) = e^{-\pi^2 t} \sin(\pi x).$$

Solution 4. We apply the Crank-Nicolson method for $c = a^2 \frac{\delta t}{\delta x^2} = (1)^2(10^{-2}/10^{-1}) = 10^{-1}$ obtained from $\delta t = 10^{-1}$, $\delta x = 10^{-2}$ values. Table 1.3 shows the Crank-Nicolson approximation results, exact solution and the error between the Crank-Nicolson and exact solution of the considered heat equation at time 0.5. We can observe from the table that the accuracy of the Crank-Nicolson method increases according to the backward finite difference method. Therefore we can generalize that the Crank-Nicolson accuracy is better for every example according to the implicit finite difference method.

1.2.4 Stability Analysis of Finite Difference Method

The problem of stability of explicit finite difference solution consists of finding conditions under which

$$w_{i,j} = \phi_{i,j} - \Phi_{i,j}$$

remains bounded as j increases.

There are two methods for stability analysis.

1. Fourier stability method (Von Neumann stability analysis)
2. Matrix method

1. **Fourier stability method (Von Neumann stability analysis)**
   Fourier stability method expresses the initial line of errors in terms of a finite Fourier Series and considers the growth of a function that reduces to this series for $t = 0$ by terms of variables separable method.

Table 1.3. The forward difference approximation results and exact solution of the heat equation

x_i	$\phi(x_i, 0.5)$	$k = 10^{-2}$	$|\phi(x_i,0.5) - \phi_{i,50}|$
0.0	0	0	0
0.1	0.230×10^{-5}	0.222×10^{-5}	6.756×10^{-5}
0.2	0.438×10^{-5}	0.422×10^{-5}	1.573×10^{-4}
0.3	0.603×10^{-5}	0.581×10^{-5}	2.165×10^{-4}
0.4	0.709×10^{-5}	0.684×10^{-5}	2.546×10^{-4}
0.5	0.745×10^{-5}	0.719×10^{-5}	2.677×10^{-4}
0.6	0.709×10^{-5}	0.684×10^{-5}	2.546×10^{-4}
0.7	0.603×10^{-5}	0.581×10^{-5}	2.165×10^{-4}
0.8	0.438×10^{-5}	0.422×10^{-5}	1.573×10^{-4}
0.9	0.230×10^{-5}	0.222×10^{-5}	8.271×10^{-5}
1.0	0	0	0

$$E(x) = \sum_{j=1} A_j e^{i\beta_j x}$$

where $|B_j|$ and j are arbitrary.

Take the errors competent $e^{\alpha t} e^{i\beta x}$. If $|e^{\alpha t}| \leq 1$ $\forall \alpha$, error will not grow. Write the explicit method for the heat equation

$$\phi_t = \phi_{xx}$$
$$\phi_{i,j+1} = (1 - 2c)\phi_{i,j} + c(\phi_{i-1,j} + \phi_{i+1,j}) \quad \phi \sim \text{Exact}$$
$$\Phi_{i,j+1} = (1 - 2c)\Phi_{m,n} + c(\Phi_{m-1,n} + \Phi_{m+1,n}) \quad \Phi \sim \text{Numerical}$$
$$z_{m,n} = \phi_{m,n} - \Phi_{m,n}$$

initially

$$z_{m,n} = \sum_{j=0}^{m} A_j e^{iB_j mh} \quad x_m = m\delta x \quad t_n = n\delta t$$
$$z_{m,n+1} = (1 - 2c)z_{m,n} + c(z_{m+1,n} + z_{m-1,n})$$
take $z_{m,n} = e^{\alpha n\delta t} e^{i\beta m\delta x} = \zeta^n e^{i\beta m\delta x} = \zeta^n \zeta^{i\beta m\delta x}$
$$z_{m,n+1} = \zeta^n \zeta^{i\beta m\delta x} = (1 - 2c)\zeta^n e^{i\beta m\delta x} + c(\zeta^n e^{i\beta(m+1)\delta x} + \zeta^n e^{i\beta(m-1)\delta x})$$

Divide by $\zeta^n e^{i\beta m\delta x}$

$$\zeta = (1 - 2c) + c(e^{i\beta\delta x} + e^{-i\beta\delta x}) = (1 - 2c) + 2c\cos(\beta\delta x)$$
$$\cos(2\theta) = 1 - 2\sin^2(\theta)$$
$$\zeta = (1 - 2c) + 2c\left(1 - 2\sin^2\left(\frac{\beta\delta x}{2}\right)\right)$$
$$= 1 - 4c\sin^2\left(\frac{\beta\delta x}{2}\right)$$

For stability

$$|1 - 4\sin^2\left(\tfrac{\beta\delta x}{2}\right)| \leq 1$$

$$-1 \leq 1 - 4c\sin^2\left(\tfrac{\beta\delta x}{2}\right) \leq 1$$

$$-2 \leq -4c\sin^2\left(\tfrac{\beta\delta x}{2}\right) \leq 0$$

$$0 \leq c\sin^2\left(\tfrac{\beta\delta x}{2}\right) \leq \tfrac{1}{2}, \text{ then}$$

$$c \leq \tfrac{1}{2}; \quad c = \tfrac{\delta t}{\delta x}$$

For implicit method,

$$\frac{\phi_{i,j+1} - \phi_{i,j}}{\delta t} = \frac{\phi_{i+1,j+1} - 2\phi_{i,j+1} + \phi_{i-1,j+1}}{\delta x^2}$$

$$c = \frac{\delta t}{\delta x^2}$$

$$(1 + 2c)\phi_{i,j+1} - c(\phi_{i+1,j+1} + \phi_{i-1,j+1}) = \phi_{i,j}$$

$$(1 + 2c)z_{m,n+1} - c(z_{m+1,n+1} + z_{m-1,n+1}) = z_{m,n}$$

$$z_{m,n} = \xi^n e^{i\beta m \delta x}$$

$$(1 + 2c)\xi^{n+1} e^{i\beta m \delta x} - c\left(\xi^{n+1} e^{i\beta(m+1)\delta x} + \xi^{n+1} e^{i\beta(m-1)\delta x}\right) = \xi^n e^{i\beta m \delta x}$$

$$\xi(1 + 2c) - c\xi(e^{i\beta\delta x} + e^{-i\beta\delta x}) = 1$$

$$\xi(1 + 2c) - c\xi(2\cos(\beta\delta x)) = 1$$

$$(1 + 2c)\xi - c\xi\left(2 - 4\sin^2\tfrac{\beta\delta x}{2}\right) = 1$$

$$\xi + 4c\xi\sin^2\left(\tfrac{\beta\delta x}{2}\right) = 1$$

$$\xi = \frac{1}{1 + 4c\sin^2\left(\tfrac{\beta\delta x}{2}\right)} \leq 1$$

2. **Matrix Method**

For the explicit method, we can write:

$$\phi_{i,j+1} = c\phi_{i-1,j} + (1 - 2c)\phi_{i,j} + c\phi_{i+1,j},$$

and we can also rewrite in the matrix-vector form:

$$\begin{bmatrix} \phi_{1,j+1} \\ \phi_{2,j+1} \\ \vdots \\ \phi_{m,j+1} \end{bmatrix} = \begin{bmatrix} 1-2c & c & 0 & \cdots & 0 \\ c & 1-2c & c & \ddots & \vdots \\ 0 & \ddots & \ddots & \ddots & 0 \\ \vdots & \ddots & \ddots & \ddots & c \\ 0 & \cdots & 0 & -c & 1+2c \end{bmatrix} \begin{bmatrix} \phi_{1,j} \\ \phi_{2,j} \\ \vdots \\ \phi_{m,j} \end{bmatrix} \quad (1.22)$$

Theorem 1. *Eigenvalues of $m \times m$ tridiagonal matrix*

$$H = \begin{bmatrix} q_1 & q_2 & \ddots & \cdots \\ & q_3 & \ddots & \ddots & \ddots \\ & & \ddots & \ddots & \ddots & \ddots \\ & & & \ddots & \ddots & \ddots \\ & & & & \ddots & \cdots & \ddots & \ddots \end{bmatrix}$$

q_2 and q_3 are real and have the same sign, and q_1 is real or complex.

$$\mu_l = q_1 + 2q_2 \sqrt{\frac{q_3}{q_2}} \cos\left(\frac{l\pi}{n+1}\right), \quad l = 1, \ldots, n$$

Eigenvalues of H : $\mu_l = (1 - 2c) + 2c\cos\left(\frac{l\pi}{n+1}\right) = 1 - 4c\sin^2\left(\frac{l\pi}{2(m+1)}\right)$

In our application the absolute eigenvalues must be less than or equal to 1. Therefore,

$$\left|1 - 4c\sin^2\left(\frac{l\pi}{2(m+1)}\right)\right| \leq 1 \quad \text{then} \quad r \leq \frac{1}{2}.$$

Stability for the Crank-Nicolson Implicit Method The Crank-Nicolson method can be written in the matrix-vector form as:

$$\begin{bmatrix} 1+2c & -c & 0 & \cdots & 0 \\ -c & \ddots & \ddots & \ddots & \vdots \\ 0 & \ddots & \ddots & \ddots & 0 \\ \vdots & \ddots & \ddots & \ddots & -c \\ 0 & \cdots & 0 & -c & 1+2c \end{bmatrix} \begin{bmatrix} \phi_{1,j+1} \\ \phi_{2,j+1} \\ \vdots \\ \phi_{m-1,j+1} \end{bmatrix}$$

$$= \begin{bmatrix} 1-2c & c & 0 & \cdots & 0 \\ c & \ddots & \ddots & \ddots & \vdots \\ 0 & \ddots & \ddots & \ddots & 0 \\ \vdots & \ddots & \ddots & \ddots & -c \\ 0 & \cdots & 0 & -c & 1+2c \end{bmatrix} \begin{bmatrix} \phi_{1,j} \\ \phi_{2,j} \\ \vdots \\ \phi_{m-1,j} \end{bmatrix} + \begin{bmatrix} bc \\ bc \\ \vdots \\ bc \end{bmatrix} \quad (1.23)$$

where bc symbolizes the boundary condition, and we can define a matrix

$$H = \begin{bmatrix} -2 & 1 & \ddots & \ddots \\ 1 & \ddots & \ddots & \ddots \\ \ddots & \ddots & \ddots & \ddots \\ \ddots & \ddots & \ddots & \ddots \\ \ddots & \cdots & \ddots & \ddots \end{bmatrix}$$

and we can rewrite the matrix-vector system of the equation as:
$$(2I - cH)\phi_{j+1} = (2I + cH)\phi_j + \beta,$$
then we can find the eigenvalues of
$$\mu_H = -2 + 2\cos\left(\frac{l\pi}{m+1}\right)$$
$$= -2 + 2\left(1 - 2\sin^2\left(\frac{l\pi}{2(m+1)}\right)\right) = -4\sin^2\left(\frac{l\pi}{2(m+1)}\right)$$

and
$$\phi_{i,j+1} = (2I - cH)^{-1}(2I + cH)\phi_{i,j} + \tilde{\beta}$$
where
$$A = (2I - cH)^{-1}(2I + cH)$$
and the eigenvalues of A is
$$\mu_A = \left|\frac{2 - 4c\sin^2\left(\frac{l\pi}{2(m+1)}\right)}{2 + 4c\sin^2\left(\frac{l\pi}{2(m+1)}\right)}\right| \leq 1$$

then we can say that the Crank-Nicolson method is unconditionally stable.

1.2.5 Exercises

Exercise 6. Find the numerical solution of the heat equation using backward difference (implicit) method
$$\frac{\partial \phi}{\partial t} - \frac{\partial^2 \phi}{\partial x^2} = 0 \quad 0 < x < 1 \quad \text{and} \quad t > 0$$
with the initial and boundary conditions
$$\phi(0, t) = \phi(1, t) = 0, \quad \phi(x, 0) = \sin(\pi x), \quad 0 < x < 1.$$

Exercise 7. Find the numerical solution of the heat equation using backward-difference (implicit) method
$$\frac{\partial \phi}{\partial t} = \frac{1}{8}\frac{\partial^2 \phi}{\partial x^2}, \quad 0 < x < 2 \quad \text{and} \quad t > 0$$
with the initial and boundary conditions
$$\phi(0, t) = \phi(2, t) = 0, \quad \phi(x, 0) = 4\sin(4\pi x), \quad 0 < x < 2$$
and compare with the exact solution of the problem.

Exercise 8. Solve the partial differential equation in Exercise 6 using Crank-Nicolson method and compare it with the exact and backward-difference solutions.

Exercise 9. Solve the partial differential equation in Exercise 7 using Crank-Nicolson method and compare it with the exact and backward-difference solutions.

Exercise 10. Find the approximate solution of the heat type partial differential equations using forward-difference method.

a. $\frac{\partial \phi}{\partial t} - \frac{\partial^2 \phi}{\partial x^2} = 0$ $0 < x < 2$ and $t > 0$ with the initial and boundary conditions $\phi(0,t) = \phi(2,t) = 0$, $\phi(x,0) = sin(2\pi x)$, $0 < x < 2$ and compare with the exact solution $\phi(x,t) = e^{-4\pi^2 t} sin(2\pi x)$ at time $t = 0.5$.

b. $\frac{\partial \phi}{\partial t} - \frac{\partial^2 \phi}{\partial x^2} = 0$ $0 < x < \pi$ and $t > 0$ with the initial and boundary conditions $\phi(0,t) = \phi(\pi,t) = 0$, $\phi(x,0) = sin(x)$, $0 < x < \pi$ and compare with the exact solution $\phi(x,t) = e^{-t} sin(x)$ at time $t = 0.5$.

Exercise 11. Find the approximate solution of the heat type partial differential equations using forward-difference method.

a. $\frac{\partial \phi}{\partial t} = \frac{1}{\pi^2} \frac{4}{\pi^2} \frac{\partial^2 \phi}{\partial x^2}$ $0 < x < 1$ and $t > 0$ with the initial and boundary conditions $\phi(0,t) = \phi(1,t) = 0$, $\phi(x,0) = cos(\pi(x - 1/2))$, $0 < x < 1$ and compare with the exact solution $\phi(x,t) = e^{-t} cos(\pi(x - 1/2)))$ at time $t = 0.5$.

b. $\frac{\partial \phi}{\partial t} = \frac{4}{\pi^2} \frac{\partial^2 \phi}{\partial x^2}$ $0 < x < 4$ and $t > 0$ with the initial and boundary conditions $\phi(0,t) = \phi(4,t) = 0$, $\phi(x,0) = sin(\frac{\pi}{4}x(1 + 2cos(\frac{\pi}{4}x)))$, $0 < x < 4$ and compare with the exact solution $\phi(x,t) = e^{-t} sin(\frac{\pi}{2}x) + e^{\frac{-t}{4}} sin(\frac{\pi}{4}x)$ at time $t = 0.5$.

Exercise 12. Solve the partial differential equation in Exercise 10 using backward-difference method.

Exercise 13. Solve the partial differential equation in Exercise 11 using backward-difference method.

Exercise 14. Solve the partial differential equation in Exercise 10 using Crank-Nicolson method.

Exercise 15. Solve the partial differential equation in Exercise 11 using Crank-Nicolson method.

Exercise 16. Find the eigenvalues of given $(n-1) \times (n-1)$ matrix H,

$$h_{i,j} = \begin{cases} \mu, & j = i-1 \text{ or } j = i+1 \\ 1 - 2\mu, & j = i \\ 0 & \text{otherwise} \end{cases}$$

are

$$\lambda_i = 1 - 4\mu \left(sin\left(\frac{i\pi}{2m}\right) \right)^2 \quad \text{for each} \quad i = 1, 2, \ldots, n-1,$$

with the corresponding eigenvectors $u^{(i)}$, where $v_j^i = sin\left(\frac{ij\pi}{m}\right)$.

Exercise 17. Find the eigenvalues of given $(n-1) \times (n-1)$ matrix H,

$$h_{i,j} = \begin{cases} -\mu, & j = i-1 \text{ or } j = i+1 \\ 1+2\mu, & j = i \\ 0 & \text{otherwise} \end{cases}$$

with the positive define $\mu > 0$, $\lambda_i = 1 + 4\mu \left(\sin\left(\frac{i\pi}{2m}\right)\right)^2$ for each $i = 1, 2, \ldots, n-1$, with the corresponding eigenvectors $u^{(i)}$, where $v_j^i = \sin\left(\frac{ij\pi}{m}\right)$.

Exercise 18. Develop the finite difference solution scheme using central difference approximation to find the approximation solution of,

$$\frac{\partial \phi}{\partial t} - \frac{\partial^2 \phi}{\partial t^2} = F(x), \quad 0 < x < l, \quad t > 0;$$
$$\phi(0,t)) = \phi(1,t) = 0 \quad t > 0;$$
$$\phi(x,0) = f(x), \quad 0 < x < l.$$

Exercise 19. Develop the finite difference solution scheme using central difference approximation to find the approximation solution of,

$$\frac{\partial \phi}{\partial t} - \frac{\partial^2 \phi}{\partial t^2} = 2, \quad 0 < x < l, \quad t > 0;$$
$$\phi(0,t)) = \phi(1,t) = 0 \quad t > 0;$$
$$\phi(x,0) = \sin(\pi x) + x(1-x), \quad 0 < x < l.$$

with $\delta x = 10^{-1}$ and $\delta t = 10^{-2}$. The exact solution of the problem is $\phi(t,x) = e^{-\pi^2 t}\sin(\pi x) + x(1-x)$. Therefore compare your solution with the exact one at $t = 0.75$.

Exercise 20. Develop the finite difference solution scheme using central difference approximation to find the approximation solution of,

$$\frac{\partial \phi}{\partial t} - \alpha^2 \frac{\partial^2 \phi}{\partial t^2} = 0, \quad 0 < x < l, \quad t > 0;$$
$$\phi(0,t)) = \varphi(t) \quad \phi(1,t) = \psi(t) \quad t > 0;$$
$$\phi(x,0) = f(x), \quad 0 < x < l.$$

where $f(0) = \varphi(0)$ and $f(l) = \psi(0)$.

Exercise 21. Develop the finite difference solution scheme using central difference approximation to find the approximation solution of,

$$\frac{\partial \phi}{\partial t} - \alpha^2 \frac{\partial^2 \phi}{\partial t^2} = 0, \quad 0 < x < l, \quad t > 0;$$
$$\phi(t,0)) = \varphi(t) \quad \phi(t,1) = \psi(t) \quad t > 0;$$
$$\phi(0,x) = f(x), \quad 0 < x < l.$$

where $f(0) = \varphi(0)$ and $f(l) = \psi(0)$.

1.3. FDM for Hyperbolic Partial Differential Equations

We will examine the approximate solution of a hyperbolic equation in this section. Therefore, we consider the wave equation which is an example of the wave equation. We can write the 1−D wave equation as:

$$\frac{\partial^2 \phi}{\partial t^2}(x,t) - \alpha^2 \frac{\partial^2 \phi}{\partial x^2}(x,t) = 0, \quad 0 < x < l, \quad t > 0; \quad (1.24)$$

with the initial and boundary conditions

$$\phi(t,0) = \phi(t,l) = 0 \quad \text{for} \quad t > 0,$$
$$\phi(0,x) = f(x), \text{ and } \frac{\partial \phi}{\partial t}(0,x) = g(x) \quad \text{for} \quad 0 \le x \le l,$$

where α is constant.

We can solve the wave equation actually by changing variables,

$$\varphi = x + t \quad \text{and} \quad \psi = x - t,$$

then, the actual solution obtained

$$\phi(t,x) = \frac{1}{2}\left[f(x+t) + f(x-t) + \int_{x-t}^{x+t} g(\rho)d\rho \right].$$

We can also solve the wave equation numerically by using the finite difference approximation.

Choose an integer $n > 0$ to determine the space step size $\delta x = l/n$ at grilling of the solution domain and also the time step size can be determined as an integer $m > 0$. Then the mesh point (x_i, t_j) can be defined

$$x_i = i\delta x \quad \text{and} \quad t_j = j\delta t,$$

for each $i = 1, 2, \ldots, n$ and $j = 1, 2, \ldots$

With any mesh point (x_i, t_j) the aforementioned equation can be written,

$$\frac{\partial^2 \phi}{\partial t^2}(x_i, t_j) - \alpha^2 \frac{\partial^2 \phi}{\partial x^2}(x_i, t_j) = 0. \quad (1.25)$$

To obtain the numerical solution of the wave equation using the finite difference method, we approximate both the time and space variables with the central difference approximation for the second derivatives of the variables,

$$\frac{\partial^2 \phi}{\partial t^2}(x_i, t_j) = \frac{\phi(x_i, t_{j+1}) - 2\phi(x_i, t_j) + \phi(x_i, t_{j-1})}{\delta t^2} - \frac{\delta t^2}{12}\frac{\partial^4 \phi}{\partial t^4}(x_i, \lambda_j),$$

where $\lambda_j \in (t_{j-1}, t_{j+1})$ and

$$\frac{\partial^2 \phi}{\partial x^2}(x_i, t_j) = \frac{\phi(x_{i+1}, t_{j-1}) - 2\phi(x_i, t_{j-1}) + \phi(x_{i-1}, t_{j-1})}{\delta t^2} - \frac{\delta x^2}{12}\frac{\partial^4 \phi}{\partial t^4}(\zeta_i, t_j),$$

or
$$\frac{\partial^2 \phi}{\partial x^2}(x_i, t_j) = \frac{\phi(x_{i+1}, t_j) - 2\phi(x_i, t_j) + \phi(x_{i-1}, t_j)}{\delta t^2} - \frac{\delta x^2}{12}\frac{\partial^4 \phi}{\partial t^4}(\zeta_i, t_j),$$

where $\zeta_i \in (x_{i-1}, x_{i+1})$.

Rewriting the quotient

$$\frac{\partial^2 \phi}{\partial t^2}(x_i, t_j) = \frac{\phi_{i,j+1} - 2\phi_{i,j} + \phi_{i,j-1}}{\delta t^2}$$

$$\frac{\partial^2 \phi}{\partial x^2}(x_i, t_j) = \frac{\phi_{i+1,j-1} - 2\phi_{i,j-1} + \phi_{i-1,j-1}}{\delta x^2}$$

or

$$\frac{\partial^2 \phi}{\partial x^2}(x_i, t_j) = \frac{\phi_{i+1,j} - 2\phi_{i,j} + \phi_{i-1,j}}{\delta x^2}$$

we obtain the wave equation in the approximate form,

$$\frac{\phi_{i,j+1} - 2\phi_{i,j} + \phi_{i,j-1}}{\delta t^2} - \alpha^2 \frac{\phi_{i+1,j} - 2\phi_{i,j} + \phi_{i-1,j}}{\delta x^2} = \frac{1}{12}\left[\delta t^2 \frac{\partial^4 \phi}{\partial t^4}(\zeta_i, t_j) - \alpha^2 \delta x^2 \frac{\partial^4 \phi}{\partial t^4}(x_i, \lambda_j)\right] \quad (1.26)$$

Disregard the error term

$$\tau_{i,j} = \frac{1}{12}\left[\delta t^2 \frac{\partial^4 \phi}{\partial t^4}(\zeta_i, t_j) - \alpha^2 \delta x^2 \frac{\partial^4 \phi}{\partial t^4}(x_i, \lambda_j)\right] \quad (1.27)$$

obtained from the difference equation

$$\frac{\phi_{i,j+1} - 2\phi_{i,j} + \phi_{i,j-1}}{\delta t^2} - \alpha^2 \frac{\phi_{i+1,j} - 2\phi_{i,j} + \phi_{i-1,j}}{\delta x^2} = 0 \quad (1.28)$$

Defining $c = \alpha \frac{\delta t}{\delta x}$, we can write the difference equation,

$$\phi_{i,j+1} - 2\phi_{i,j} + \phi_{i,j-1} - c^2 \phi_{i+1,j} + 2c^2 \phi_{i,j} - c^2 \phi_{i-1,j} = 0$$

and then solve to find $\phi_{i,j+1}$

$$\phi_{i,j+1} = 2(1 - c^2)\phi_{i,j} + c^2(\phi_{i+1,j} + \phi_{i-1,j}) - \phi_{i,j-1},$$

for each $i = 1, 2, \ldots, n-1$ and $j = 1, 2, \ldots$. The boundary condition discretizes as:

$$\phi_{1,j} = \phi_{n,j} = 0 \quad \text{for each} \quad j = 1, 2, 3, \ldots,$$

and the initial condition discretizes as:

$$\phi_{i,1} = f(x_i) \quad \text{for each} \quad i = 1, 2, 3, \ldots, m-1.$$

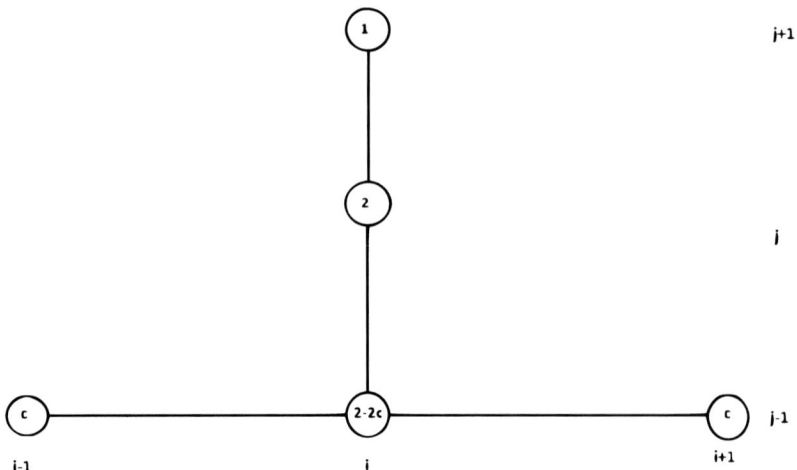

Figure 1.7. Computational molecule of 1D wave equation with explicit finite difference method

$$\begin{bmatrix} \phi_{1,j+1} \\ \phi_{2,j+1} \\ \vdots \\ \phi_{m-1,j+1} \end{bmatrix} = \begin{bmatrix} 2(1-c^2) & c^2 & 0 & \cdots & 0 \\ c^2 & 2(1-c^2) & v & & \vdots \\ 0 & \ddots & \ddots & \ddots & 0 \\ \vdots & & \ddots & \ddots & c \\ 0 & \cdots & 0 & c^2 & 2(1-c^2) \end{bmatrix} \begin{bmatrix} \phi_{1,j} \\ \phi_{2,j} \\ \vdots \\ \phi_{m-1,j} \end{bmatrix} - \begin{bmatrix} \phi_{1,j-1} \\ \phi_{2,j-1} \\ \vdots \\ \phi_{m-1,j-1} \end{bmatrix} \quad (1.29)$$

In the solution procedure, we have to consider the known and unknown terms at $j-1, j$ and $j+1$ time levels. At the $j-1$st time level, there is a minor problem because we start with $j = 1$ and $j-1$ becomes 0, but we do not know the values at this time step. Therefore, we must use

$$\frac{\partial \phi}{\partial t}(0, x) = g(x), \quad 0 \le x \le 1$$

to acquire it.

Using the forward-difference approximation, we can get

$$\frac{\partial \phi}{\partial t} = \frac{\phi_{x_i} - \phi_{0,x_i,t_1}}{\delta t} = g(x)$$

and obtaining for $\phi(x_i, t_1)$ in the equality, we get

$$\phi_{x_i,t_1} = \phi(x_i, 0) + \delta t g(x_i) \quad \text{for each} \quad i = 1, 2, \ldots, m-1.$$

Then, we can write the computational molecules of the explicit, implicit and Crank-Nicolson finite difference method, respectively.

If we consider the $j+1$th time step for the second derivative for the space variable, we will obtain the computational molecule as:

$$\phi_{xx} = \frac{\phi_{i+1,j+1} - \phi_{i,j+1} + \phi_{i-1,j+1}}{\delta x^2}$$

If we consider the average of the $j-1$th and $j+1$th time step for the second derivative for

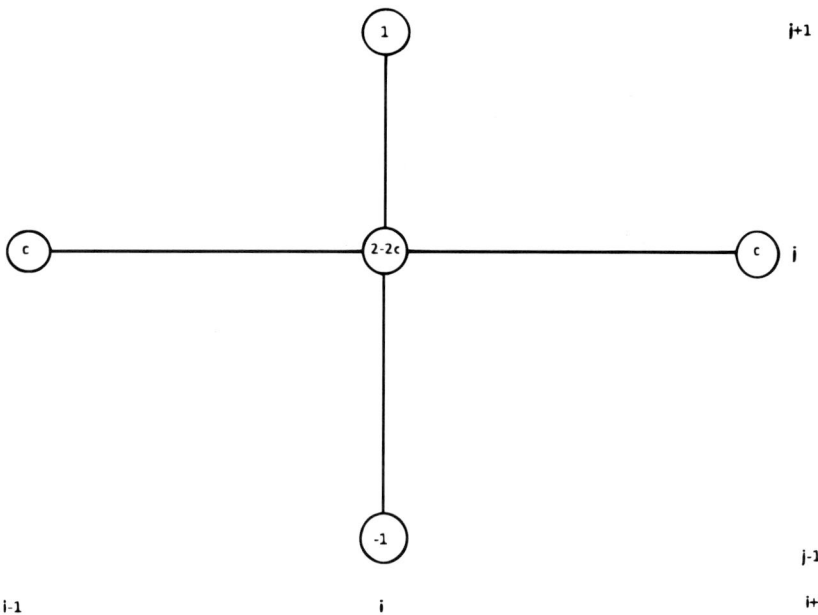

Figure 1.8. Computational molecule of 1D wave equation with explicit finite difference method

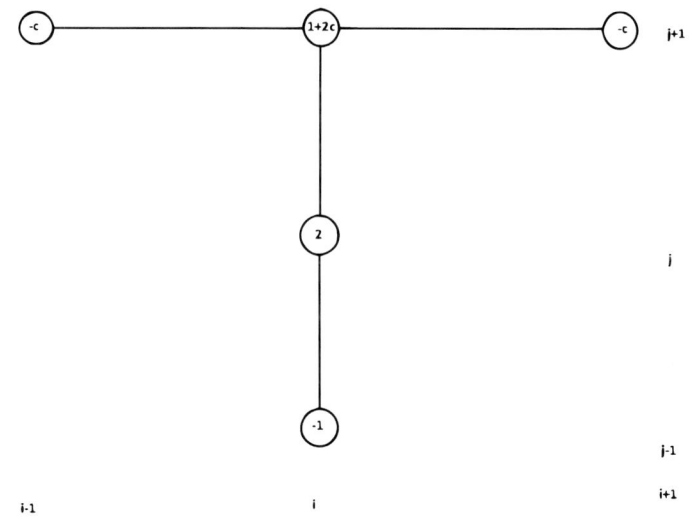

Figure 1.9. Computational molecule of 1D wave equation with implicit finite difference method

the space variable,

$$\phi_{xx} = \frac{1}{2}\left[\frac{\phi_{i+1,j+1} - \phi_{i,j+1} + \phi_{i-1,j+1}}{\delta x^2} + \frac{\phi_{i+1,j-1} - \phi_{i,j-1} + \phi_{i-1,j-1}}{\delta x^2}\right]$$

we will obtain the computational molecule as:

Exercise 22. Solve the hyperbolic problem using the finite difference approximation

$$\frac{\partial^2 \phi}{\partial t^2}(x,t) - 4\frac{\partial^2 \phi}{\partial x^2}(x,t) = 0, \quad 0 < x < 1, \quad t > 0,$$

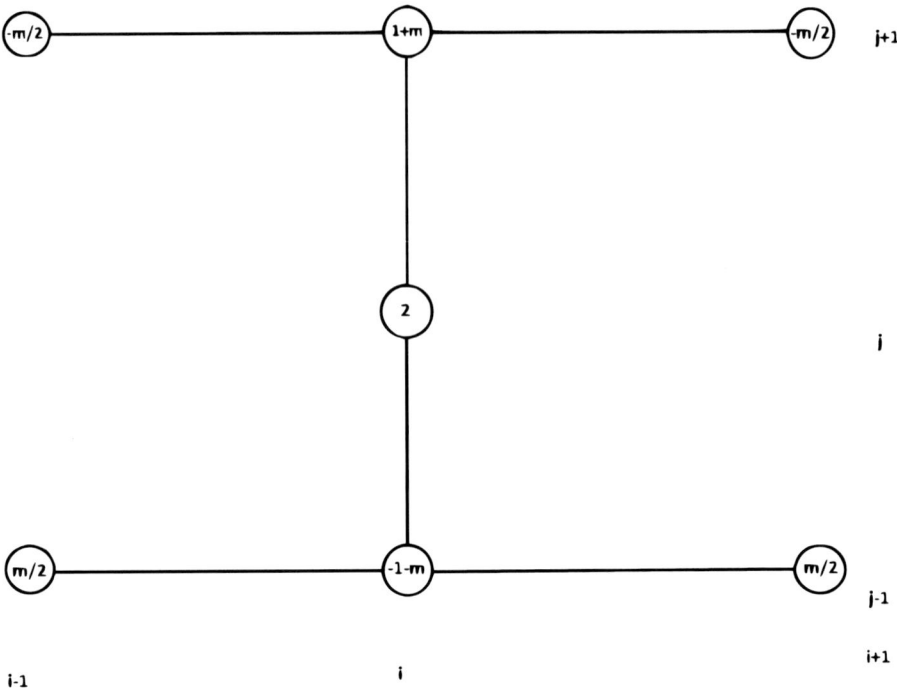

Figure 1.10. Computational molecule of 1D wave equation with Crank-Nicolson finite difference method

with boundary conditions

$$\phi(0, t) = \phi(1, t) = 0, \quad \text{for} \quad t > 0,$$

and initial conditions

$$\phi(x, 0) = sin(\pi x), \quad 0 \leq x \leq 1, \quad \text{and} \quad \frac{\partial u}{\partial t}(x, 0) = 0, \quad 0 \leq x \leq 1,$$

and compare the approximate results with the actual solution

$$\phi(x, t) = cos(2\pi t)sin(\pi x).$$

Solution 5. To find the approximate solution we take $\delta x = 0.1$ and $\delta t = 0.001$. We can say from the Taylor series expansion is that the truncation error $O(\delta t^2 + \delta x^2)$. We can write the finite difference approximation for the wave equation as:

$$\frac{\phi_{i,j+1} - 2\phi_{i,j} + \phi_{i,j-1}}{\delta t^2} = 4\frac{\phi_{i+1,j} - 2\phi_{i,j} + \phi_{i-1,j}}{\delta x^2}$$

we can assign $c = 4\frac{\delta t^2}{\delta x^2}$, then we can write

$$\phi_{i,j+1} = 4c\phi_{i+1,j} + (2 - 8c)\phi_{i,j} + 4c\phi_{i-1,j} - \phi_{i-1,j}$$

then we use the initial conditions using central difference approximation as:

Table 1.4. Grid points and numerical solutions at time=0.2

x_i	ϕ_i
0	0
0.1	0.30901
0.2	0.58779
0.3	0.80901
0.4	0.95106
0.5	1.00000
0.6	0.95106
0.7	0.80901
0.8	0.58779
0.9	0.30902
1.0	0.00000

$$\frac{\partial \phi}{\partial t}(x,0) = g(x)$$

$$\frac{\phi_{i+1,j} - \phi_{i-1,j}}{2\delta t} = g(x)$$

$$\phi_{i-1,j} = \phi_{i+1,j} - 2\delta t g(x)$$

and using this equality, we obtain the scheme,

$$\phi_{i,j+1} = 4c\phi_{i+1,j} + (2 - 8c)\phi_{i,j} + 4c\phi_{i-1,j} - \phi_{i+1,j} + 2\delta t g(x)$$

1.3.1 Stability Analysis

We define

$$E_{p,q} = e^{i\beta p \delta x}$$

similar to the heat equation. For stability the condition $|\xi| < 1$ must be satisfied.

$$e^{i\beta p \delta x}\xi^{q+1} = -e^{i\beta p \delta x}\xi^{q-1} + m\xi^q(e^{i\beta(p-1)\delta x} + e^{i\beta(p+1)\delta x}) + 2(1-m)e^{i\beta p \delta x}\xi^q$$

then we obtain

$$\xi^2 = -1 + m\xi(e^{-i\beta \delta x} + e^{i\beta \delta x}) + 2(1-m)\xi$$

$$\xi^2 + 1 - 2\xi + m\xi(1 - e^{i\beta \delta x} - e^{-i\beta \delta x}) = 0$$

$$\xi^2 + 1 - 2\xi + m\xi(1 - 2\cos(\beta \delta x)) = 0$$

$$\xi^2 + 1 - 2\xi + m\xi\left(1 - 2 + 4\sin^2\left(\frac{\beta \delta x}{2}\right)\right) = 0$$

$$\xi^2 + 1 - 2\xi\left(1 - 2m\sin^2\left(\frac{\beta \delta x}{2}\right)\right) = 0.$$

Then we can find the root of ξ by solving the last equation as:

$$\xi_{1,2} = \frac{2\left(1 - 2m\sin^2\left(\frac{\beta\delta x}{2}\right)\right) \mp \sqrt{4\left(1 - 2m\sin^2\left(\frac{\beta\delta x}{2}\right)\right)^2 - 4}}{2}$$

$$= 1 - 2m\sin^2\left(\frac{\beta\delta x}{2}\right) \mp \sqrt{\left(1 - 2m\sin^2\left(\frac{\beta\delta x}{2}\right)\right)^2 - 1}$$

then

$$\xi_1 = 1 - 2m\sin^2\left(\frac{\beta\delta x}{2}\right) + \sqrt{\left(1 - 2m\sin^2\left(\frac{\beta\delta x}{2}\right)\right)^2 - 1}$$

$$\xi_2 = 1 - 2m\sin^2\left(\frac{\beta\delta x}{2}\right) - \sqrt{\left(1 - 2m\sin^2\left(\frac{\beta\delta x}{2}\right)\right)^2 - 1}$$

for stability both $|\xi_1|$ and $|\xi_2|$ must be less than 1. Therefore

$$-1 \leq x \leq 1$$
$$-1 \leq 1 - 2m\sin^2\left(\frac{\beta\delta x}{2}\right) \leq 1$$
$$-2 \leq -2m\sin^2(\beta\delta x) \leq 0$$
$$0 \leq m\sin^2\left(\frac{\beta\delta x}{2}\right) \leq 1$$
$$m\frac{\delta t^2}{\delta x^2} \leq 1$$
$$\frac{\delta t}{\delta x} \leq 1.$$

Exercise 23. Find the solution of the wave equation using finite difference approximation

$$\frac{\partial^2 \phi}{\partial t^2} - \frac{\partial^2 \phi}{\partial x^2} = 0, \quad 0 < x < 1, \quad t > 0,$$
$$\phi(0, t) = \phi(1, t) = 0, \quad t > 0,$$
$$\phi(x, 0) = \sin(\pi/2 x), \quad 0 < x < 1,$$
$$\frac{\partial \phi}{\partial t}(x, 0) = 0, \quad 0 < x < 1,$$

using the finite difference method and compare with the exact solution.

Exercise 24. Find the solution of the wave equation using finite difference approximation

$$\frac{\partial^2 \phi}{\partial t^2} - \frac{1}{16\pi^2}\frac{\partial^2 \phi}{\partial x^2} = 0, \quad 0 < x < 2, \quad t > 0,$$
$$\phi(0, t) = \phi(2, t) = 0, \quad t > 0,$$
$$\phi(x, 0) = 0, \quad 0 < x < 2,$$
$$\frac{\partial \phi}{\partial t}(x, 0) = \sin(\pi x), \quad 0 < x < 2,$$

using the finite difference method and compare with the exact solution.

Exercise 25. Find the solution of the wave equation using finite difference approximation

$$\frac{\partial^2 \phi}{\partial t^2} - \frac{1}{16\pi^2}\frac{\partial^2 \phi}{\partial x^2} = 0, \quad 0 < x < \pi/2, \quad t > 0,$$
$$\phi(0, t) = \phi(\pi/2, t) = 0, \quad t > 0,$$
$$\phi(x, 0) = \sin(\pi x), \quad 0 < x < \pi/2,$$
$$\frac{\partial \phi}{\partial t}(x, 0) = 0, \quad 0 < x < \pi/2,$$

using the finite difference method and compare with the exact solution.

Exercise 26. Find the solution of the wave equation using finite difference approximation

$$\frac{\partial^2 \phi}{\partial t^2} - \frac{\partial^2 \phi}{\partial x^2} = 0, \quad 0 < x < \pi/2, \quad t > 0,$$
$$\phi(0, t) = \phi(\pi/2, t) = 0, \quad t > 0,$$
$$\phi(x, 0) = \sin(\pi x), \quad 0 < x < \pi/2,$$
$$\frac{\partial \phi}{\partial t}(x, 0) = 0, \quad 0 < x < \pi/2,$$

using the finite difference method and compare with the exact solution.

Exercise 27. Find the solution of the wave equation using finite difference approximation

$$\frac{\partial^2 \phi}{\partial t^2} - \frac{\partial^2 \phi}{\partial x^2} = 0, \quad 0 < x < 1, \quad t > 0,$$
$$\phi(0, t) = \phi(1, t) = 0, \quad t > 0,$$
$$\phi(x, 0) = \begin{cases} -x, & 0 < x < \frac{1}{2} \\ x, & \frac{1}{2} < x < 1 \end{cases}, \quad 0 < x < 1,$$
$$\frac{\partial \phi}{\partial t}(x, 0) = 0, \quad 0 < x < 1,$$

using the finite difference method and compare with the exact solution.

Exercise 28. Find the solution of the wave equation using finite difference approximation

$$\frac{\partial^2 \phi}{\partial t^2} - \frac{\partial^2 \phi}{\partial x^2} = 0, \quad 0 < x < 1, \quad t > 0,$$
$$\phi(0, t) = \phi(1, t) = 0, \quad t > 0,$$
$$\phi(x, 0) = \begin{cases} \frac{x}{4}, & 0 < x < \frac{1}{2} \\ \frac{1-x}{4}, & \frac{1}{2} < x < 1 \end{cases}, \quad 0 < x < 1,$$
$$\frac{\partial \phi}{\partial t}(x, 0) = 0, \quad 0 < x < 1,$$

using the finite difference method and compare with the exact solution.

Chapter 2

Finite Element Method for the Solution of Partial Differential Equations (PDE)

2.1. The Development of the Finite Element Method

In this section, the information about Finite Element Method (FEM), which is used in solving many physical and mathematical problems, especially engineering problems, will be given. The finite element method is an effective numerical method used for solving problems modeled with differential equations. The finite element method is a numerical method in which problems defined in complex or large regions are divided into simpler subregions and an approximate solution to the exact solution is obtained from the combination of the solutions obtained under more flexible conditions in each subregion. The Finite Element Method has three basic features:

1. First, the geometrically complex solution region is subdivided into geometrically simpler subregions called finite elements. These subregions are called "Elements." The connection between the elements is provided by points called nodes.
2. Secondly, the solution in each element is defined as continuous function also among the elements formed by the linear combination of algebraic polynomials.
3. Finally, the unknown functions are obtained by solving the equations defined on each element at certain points. The approximation functions used are usually chosen from polynomials. The degree of the selected polynomials depends on the degree of the defining equation of the problem to be solved and the number of discretization points in the element to be solved. In the finite element method, element-wise unknowns are the values of the solution of the equation at the discretization points.

Although the finite element method is perceived as a new numerical solution method, its use dates back to ancient times. The first use of the finite element method was in the field of geometry two thousand years ago. Ancient geometers used the finite element method to approximate π and calculate the area and perimeter of a circle. In the circle example, solving the simplified problem by dividing the circle into regular polygons shows the important characteristic of the finite element method. The prevalence and success of the finite element method has increased and become widespread with the rapid development of the computer.

The finite element method has been used in the field of structural analysis in the modern sense. The studies of Alexander Hrennikoff and McHenry in which they developed semi-analytical analysis methods are the first in this field. Hrennikoff and Henry used one-dimensional line elements for stress solutions. Richard Courant proposed to use stress solutions in a variational form. Then, Courant introduced piecewise shape functions on the sub-triangular regions that form the whole domain of the problem to obtain approximate numerical solutions. Levy developed the flexible (also called force) method in 1947. The equations that Levy obtained with this method were not preferred much since they were easily solved analytically. However, with the development of computer software, the method suggested by Levy started to be used. Argyis and Kelsey (1954) developed the "matrix structural analysis" method using the energy principle. This development enabled the energy principle to play an important role in the finite element method. Turner et al. conducted studies on two-dimensional elements. They created the element matrix (rigidity matrix) for the truss element, beam element and two-dimensional triangular and rectangular elements. The term "finite elements" was first used by Ray W. Clough (1960) when it began to be applied to the planar stress analysis of triangular and rectangular elements. The application of the finite element method to three-dimensional problems was easily realized after the two-dimensional theory. Melosh developed the element matrix of the regular curved rectangular plate element. The first real shell elements were axial and symmetrical elements and were used in three-dimensional structural analysis. These shell elements were followed by cylindrical and other shell elements. In the early 1960s, nonlinear problems began to be dealt with. Turner et al. developed a solution technique for geometrically nonlinear problems. Stability analysis with the finite element method was first studied by Martin. Later on, besides static problems, dynamic problems started to be studied with the finite element method. In 1943, Richard Courant solved a torsion problem using the regional continuous linear approach.

The solution to problems outside the field of construction with the finite element method started in the 1960s. Olgierd Zienkiewicz and Cheung (1965) solved Poisson's differential equation using the finite element method. Doctors also applied the finite element method to potential flow. The term "variational formulation," which is frequently used in the finite element method, was first used by Melosh, and the application of the "weighted residue method" in the finite element method was carried out by Szabo and Lee. Later, the finite element method was developed and used to solve problems in heat transfer, groundwater flow, magnetic field and many other fields. Since the 1970s, general-purpose finite element packages have begun to emerge. Today, there are many commercial finite element analysis packages such as Ansys, Abaqus, Adina, COMSOL Multiphysics, Nastran, Sap 2000 and open-source software such as FreeFEM, Calculix, Elmer, GetFEM++ and OOFEM. In addition, thousands of articles and many books have been published on the finite element method and its applications. The finite element method is also developed in line with advancing computer technology, and more efficient and faster methods are realized.

2.2. Application of Finite Element Method to Partial Differential Equations

In this section, the application of the finite element method to partial differential equations will be examined. The steps to be followed at this stage are:

- Division of the region into finite elements.
- Obtaining the weak or weighted integral formulation.
- Selection of shape functions.
- Development of finite element method over weak form.
- Placing the equations obtained in the sub-element matrix into the main matrix.
- Application of boundary conditions.
- Solution of the obtained algebraic equation system.

2.2.1 Discretization

One of the first and most important steps of the finite element problem is to determine the element type and to divide the solution region of the problem into subregions (elements) according to the type of the determined element. The discretization of the domain of the problem affects the amount of memory required to solve the problem, the processing time and the convergence of the approximate solution. The most suitable element type should be used for the solution region of the problem. In addition to the element type, the dimensions and number of elements should also be chosen in such a way as to best represent the described problem and minimize computations. For example, if the function changes abruptly in certain regions, the elements should be chosen more densely in these regions. The numerical solution, the results to be obtained in the ratio of the selected elements to represent the solution region, will be close to the real solution. As well as choosing the appropriate element, the locations of these elements and their discretization points (node points) and the numbering order of these nodes are among the factors affecting the convergence of the numerical results to be obtained. The discretization of a region for its solution with the finite element method is the division of the region into smaller and simpler subregions. Thus, an approximate solution to the solution of the original problem is obtained by combining the solutions obtained with the simple approaches made on each subregion of the discretizing problem.

2.2.2 Elements

In the finite element method, the domain of the problem is divided into simpler sub-regions called elements (discrete operation). These elements are connected to each other at certain points. These points are called nodes. Apart from the node points, points can be selected on the edges of the element or inside the element. All these selected points and nodes are called discretization points.

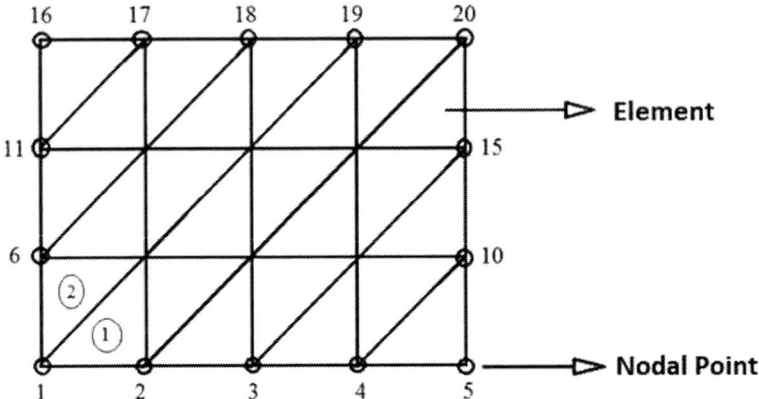

Figure 2.1. Numbering order of discretization points

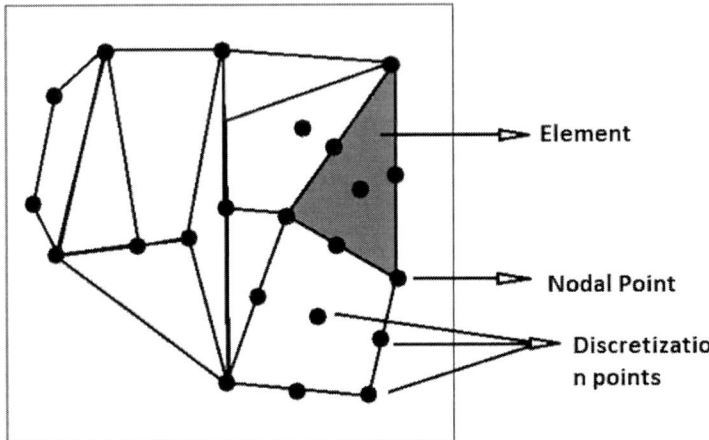

Figure 2.2. Discretization points and elements in a finite element model

2.2.3 2-D Elements

Triangle and quadrilateral-type elements are generally preferred in two-dimensional space. The basic element of this group is the triangular element with three nodes. Six, nine or more split points can also be selected on the triangular element. The number of discretization points is determined by the degree of the shape function to be selected. Since non-uniform regions can be decomposed into smoother and geometrically simpler sub-regions, triangular elements are often used in the discretization of such regions. For these reasons, the triangular element is the more useful and preferred element type. If the discretization points are taken only at the vertices of the triangle, this type of triangular element is called a linear triangular element, and if the discretization points are chosen to be at the vertices of the triangle and one point on each side, this type of element is called a quadratic triangular element. The rectangular element, on the other hand, is the preferred element type in problems where the definition region is suitable for the geometric structure. A rectangular element can also have four or more discretization points. A rectangular element is chosen as a rectangular element, which is a special case, if the problem region has a regular structure.

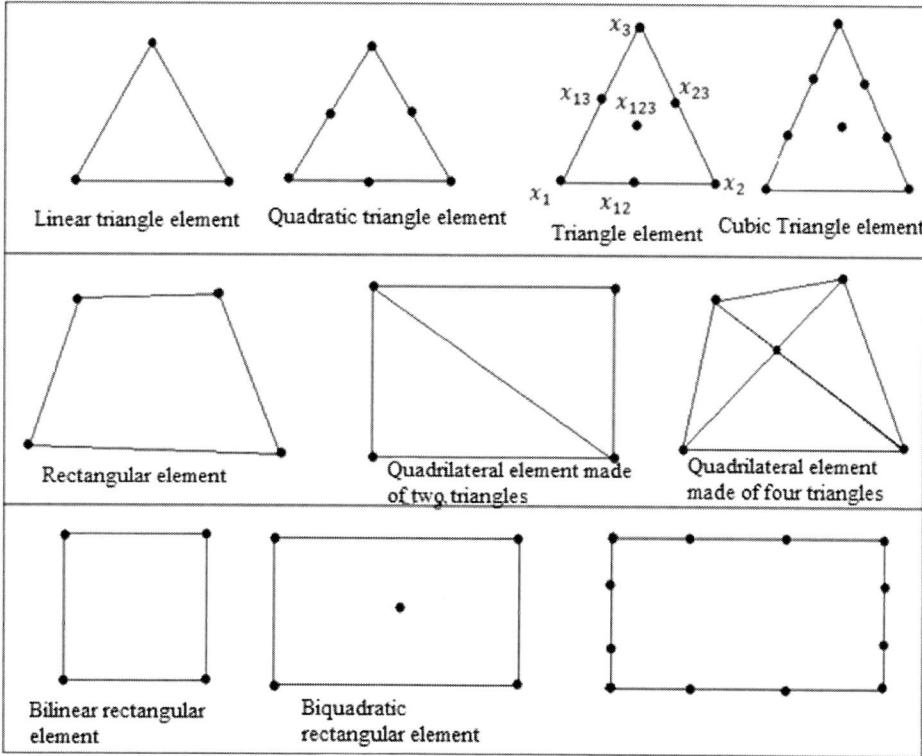

Figure 2.3. Discretization points and elements in a finite element model

2.2.4 Shape Functions

In the finite element method, the unknown function is the linear (linear) combination of the shape functions N_i defined at the discretization points selected on the element obtained by discretization of the region. The unknown function $\phi(x)$ on element e is approximately $\phi_h^e(x)$ using the $\phi_i^e(x)$ values at the nodes

$$\phi(x) \approx \phi_h^e(x) = \sum_{i=1}^{n} \phi_i^e N_i^e(x) \tag{2.1}$$

defined in the form. The properties and selection of shape functions in two-dimensional space and the shape functions used in this study are introduced below.

2.2.5 Triangular Elements Shape Functions

The first step in modeling with triangular elements is the discretization of the solution region with triangles. The main condition to be considered while discretization is that the region is divided into triangles without any gaps and that the triangles do not overlap each other. In standard discretization, triangles must be connected to each other by their vertices. Well the vertex of one triangle should not come to the side of another triangle. In addition to these basic conditions, there are other conditions that affect the convergence of the numerical solution to the real solution. Choosing triangles close to equilateral triangles ensures that the numerical solution is closer to the real solution. The smaller the interior angle of the triangles, the greater the error between the numerical solution and the real solution. Instead of reducing the interior angle of the triangle, using a triangle with more than one dimension but a larger interior angle for the same region allows us to obtain a numerical solution if we are closer to the real solution. Corner points are used to define triangles. The vertices of the triangles form the nodal points. Therefore, a triangular element has three nodes and three edges. When writing the vertices of the triangles, the same rotation direction should be used for all triangles. This direction of rotation must be either clockwise or counterclockwise. When writing the corner points of a triangle, you can start from the desired corner. The point to be considered is that no matter which point one starts from, the other two points must be selected according to the direction of rotation used. In accordance with these rules, the region is discretized into triangles. The shape functions to be used are determined by selecting points on each triangle.

The dimensionless linear (linear) shape functions obtained on the unit triangle in the range of $[0, 1] \times [0, 1]$ by considering only the vertices of the triangle used in this study are as follows:

$$\begin{aligned} N_1(\xi, \eta) &= \xi \\ N_2(\xi, \eta) &= \eta \\ N_3(\xi, \eta) &= 1 - \xi - \eta. \end{aligned} \quad (2.2)$$

2.2.6 Finite Element Method Formulation for Laplace Equation

While obtaining the finite element method formulation, first the strong form of the problem is reduced to the weak form. Then, the variational form is obtained over the weak form of the problem.

2.2.7 Weak Form for Laplace Equation

First, let's define some function spaces.

$$L^2(\Omega) = \left\{ \phi : \Omega \to \mathbb{R} \mid \int_\Omega |\phi(x)|^2 dx < |\infty \right\}$$

$$H^1(\Omega) = \left\{ \phi : \in L^2(\Omega) \mid \phi' \in L^2(\Omega) \right\}$$

$$V = H_0^1(\Omega) = \left\{ \phi : \in H^1(\Omega) \mid \phi = 0 \partial \Omega \right\}$$

where
$L^2(\Omega)$: the space of quadratic integrable functions in the region Ω
$H^1(\Omega)$: the subspace of $L^2(\Omega)$
$V = H_0^1(\Omega)$; $H^1(\Omega)$ represents the subspace of the Ω space that takes a zero value at the Ω boundary. For $\phi \in V$, which provides the strong form of the given differential

Finite Element Method for the Solution of Partial Differential Equations (PDE)

equation, the strong case of the problem is written in homogeneous form. Then the equation is multiplied by a weight (test) function w and integrated over the domain of the problem and set to zero. This method is called the weighted residual method.

The Laplace equation for the unknown function $\phi(x, y)$ from the type of boundary conditions of Dirichlet and Neumann type in two-dimensional space is expressed as follows.

$$\begin{cases} \nabla^2 \phi(x,y) = 0 & (x,y) \in \Omega \\ \phi(x,y)|_{(x,y) \in \Omega} = \phi_0, & (x,y) \in \partial\Omega_1 \\ \phi(x,y)|_{(x,y) \in \Omega} = q_0, & (x,y) \in \partial\Omega_2 \end{cases} \quad (2.3)$$

If the weighted residue method over the Ω region is applied to the Laplace equation with Ω weight function in two-dimensional space, firstly we obtain

$$\int_\Omega (\nabla^2 \phi) w \, d\Omega = 0 \quad (2.4)$$

Then applying the divergence theorem in equation (2.4), we obtain

$$\int_\Omega (\nabla^2 \phi) w \, d\Omega = -\int_\Omega \nabla \phi \nabla w \, d\Omega + \oint_{\partial\Omega_2} (\vec{n} \nabla \phi) w \, ds = 0 \quad (2.5)$$

where $\vec{n} = (n_x, n_y)$, $\partial\Omega$ is the unit normal vector on the boundary $\partial\Omega$.

We can rewrite equation (2.5) considering the

$$\vec{n} \nabla \phi = q_n = (n_x, n_y) . \begin{bmatrix} \frac{\partial \phi}{\partial x} \\ \frac{\partial \phi}{\partial y} \end{bmatrix} = \frac{\partial \phi}{\partial x} n_x + \frac{\partial \phi}{\partial y} n_y$$

as:

$$\int_\Omega \nabla \phi \nabla w \, d\Omega - \oint_{\partial\Omega_2} q_n w \, ds = 0. \quad (2.6)$$

If the obtained integral can be rewritten for the area integral in the bilinear form

$$a(\phi, w) = \int_\Omega (\phi, w) \, d\Omega$$

and in the linear form for the boundary integral

$$\ell(q_n, w) = \int_{\partial\Omega_2} (q_n, w) \, d\Omega$$

the weak form of the equation can be written as:

$$a(\nabla \phi, \nabla w) - \ell(q_n, w) = 0. \quad (2.7)$$

Equation (2.7) is named the weak form of equation (2.5).

The reasons why the weak form of the problem is needed are the following:

- Derivative order decreases by one degree.
- This one-degree decrease in the derivative order will make it sufficient for the selected shape functions to be differentiable in the first order.

- It is expected to satisfy the condition that the weak state of the equation is provided only at the nodal points.

Because of these elasticities in the numerical solution (2.7), it is called the weak form of the equation. However, while the strong form of the equation also satisfies the weak form, the weak form need not satisfy the strong form.

2.2.8 Variational Form for Laplace Equation

The unknown function ϕ is defined in a discrete form on each element of the Ω domain as:

$$\phi(x) \approx \phi_h^e(x) = \sum_{i=1}^{n} \phi_i^e N_i^e(x)$$

where $\delta_{i,j}$ is the Kronecker delta function and linear shape function $N_i^e(x)$ can be defined as:

$$N_i^e(x_j) = \delta_{i,j} = \begin{cases} 1, & i = j \\ 0, & i \neq j \end{cases}$$

In order for the approximate solution to converge to the real solution, the following conditions are specified on the $\phi_h^e(x)$ approximation:

- $\phi_h^e(x)$ must be continuous on each element and at the connection points of the elements.
- Base polynomials must consist of terms, each of which is linearly independent.
- Polynomials representing the $\phi_h^e(x)$ approximation must be complete.

The integral equation obtained by substituting the finite element approach in the weak case of the problem is calculated on each subregion where the definition (solution) region of the problem is discretized. The integral equation we obtain as a result of these operations is called the variational (discrete) version of the problem.

Writing the approximation (2.1) instead of function ϕ in the finite element method formulation in equation (2.7), we obtain the integral equation

$$\int_{\Omega_e} \left\{ \frac{\partial w}{\partial x} \sum_{i=1}^{n} \phi_i^e \frac{\partial N_i^e}{\partial x} + \frac{\partial w}{\partial y} \sum_{i=1}^{n} \phi_i^e \frac{\partial N_i^e}{\partial y} \right\} dxdy - \oint_{\partial \Omega} q_n w ds = 0 \qquad (2.8)$$

The form of the problem in (2.8) is called the discretized form of the problem on each element. In the Galerkin method, the weight function w can also be called a linear combination of shape functions. The weight function can be written as the form of shape functions in

$$\nabla w = \sum_{j=1}^{n} \left(\frac{\partial N_j^e}{\partial x}, \frac{\partial N_j^e}{\partial y} \right) \quad \text{and} \quad \nabla \phi = \left(\frac{\partial N_i^e}{\partial x}, \frac{\partial N_i^e}{\partial y} \right) \qquad (2.9)$$

The variational form of the problem can be written using bilinear and linear forms as:

$$a(\nabla \phi_h, \nabla w_h) - \ell(q_n, w_h) = 0.$$

In more detail, using the expressions in (2.9) in (2.8), the algebraic equations for the unknown function values at the nodes on the jth element are obtained as follows:

$$\int_{\Omega_e} \left\{ \left(\sum_{i=1}^{n} \frac{\partial N_j^e}{\partial x} \frac{\partial N_i^e}{\partial x} + \frac{\partial N_j^e}{\partial y} \frac{\partial N_i^e}{\partial y} \right) \phi_i^e \right\} dxdy - \oint_{\partial \Omega} q_n N_j^e ds = 0 \quad j = 1, 2, \ldots, n \quad (2.10)$$

or

$$\sum_{i=1}^{n} \left\{ \int_{\Omega_e} \left(\frac{\partial N_j^e}{\partial x} \frac{\partial N_i^e}{\partial x} + \frac{\partial N_j^e}{\partial y} \frac{\partial N_i^e}{\partial y} \right) dxdy \right\} \phi_i^e - \oint_{\partial \Omega} q_n N_j^e ds = 0 \quad j = 1, 2, \ldots, n \quad (2.11)$$

Define the following definition to group the terms in equation (2.11)

$$K_{ij}^e = \int_{\Omega_e} \left(\frac{\partial N_j^e}{\partial x} \frac{\partial N_i^e}{\partial x} + \frac{\partial N_j^e}{\partial y} \frac{\partial N_i^e}{\partial y} \right) dxdy$$

$$Q_j^e = \oint_{\partial \Omega} q_n N_j^e ds$$

Then using these terms in the (2.11), we obtain the system of equations as:

$$\sum_{i=1}^{n} K_{ij}^e \phi_i^e = Q_j^e \quad j = 1, 2, \ldots, n \quad (2.12)$$

the system of equations (2.12) can be rewritten

$$[K^e]\{\phi^e\} = \{Q^e\}. \quad (2.13)$$

In equation (2.13), $[K^e]$ matrix represents the $n \times n$ type, positive definite and symmetric element matrix, and $\{Q^e\}$ represents the $n \times 1$ type element vector.

For each element, the element matrix and vector are calculated. By using the obtained element matrices and vectors, the effects of the points on the elements to each other are effected on the big (main) system corresponding to all the unknowns in the problem solution region (global assembly procedure). The resulting large system is expressed as follows.

$$[K]\{u\} = \{Q\} \quad (2.14)$$

Boundary conditions are applied to the system before solving the large system.

Chapter 3

The Numerical Integration Methods

The integration cannot be calculated analytically due to the structure of the function, e.g.,

$$\int_0^1 \frac{e^x}{x}dx, \quad \int_0^1 e^{x^2}dx, \quad \int_0^1 \sin\left(x^2\right)dx, \quad \int_0^1 \sin\left(e^{x^2}\right)dx \tag{3.1}$$

We can calculate the integration numerically for certain points of the $f(x)$ function.

3.1. Newton-Type Integration Methods

3.1.1 Trapezium Rule

$$\int_a^b f(x)dx \approx \frac{b-a}{2}(f(a)+f(b)) \tag{3.2}$$

then divide (a,b) to the n point $a = x_0 < x_1 < \ldots < x_n = b$

$$\int_a^b f(x)dx \approx \sum_{i=1}^n (x_i - x_{i-1})f(x_{i-1}) \; (left) \tag{3.3}$$

$$\int_a^b f(x)dx \approx \sum_{i=1}^n (x_i - x_{i-1})f(x_i) \; (right) \tag{3.4}$$

$$\int_a^b f(x)dx \approx \sum_{i=1}^n (x_i - x_{i-1})\left(\frac{f(x_i)+f(x_{i-1})}{2}\right) \; (trapezium) \tag{3.5}$$

In: Higgs Boson: A Mathematical Survey with Finite Element Method
Editors: Harun Selvitopi
ISBN: 979-8-88697-785-1
© 2023 Nova Science Publishers, Inc.

3.1.2 Simpson Method

$$\int_a^b f(x)dx \approx \frac{b-a}{4}\left[f(a) + 2f\left(\frac{a+b}{2}\right) + f(b)\right]$$

$$\approx \frac{b-a}{8}[f(x_0) + 3f(x_1) + 3f(x_2) + f(x_3)] \quad (3.6)$$

$$\approx \frac{b-a}{16}[f(x_0) + 4f(x_1) + 6f(x_2) + 4f(x_3) + f(x_4)]$$

3.2. Gauss-Type Integration Methods

3.2.1 Gauss-Legendre Method

$$x; [a, b] \to [1, 1]$$
$$x = ct + d \quad (3.7)$$

$$a = -c + d$$
$$b = c + d$$

then

$$d = \frac{b+a}{2}$$
$$c = \frac{b-a}{2}$$

then we obtain

$$x = \frac{b-a}{2}t + \frac{b+a}{2} \quad (3.8)$$

$$\int_a^b f(x)dx = \int_{-1}^{1} f\left(\frac{b-a}{2}t + \frac{b+a}{2}\right)\left(\frac{b-a}{2}\right)dx$$

$$= \int_{-1}^{1} g(t)dt$$

$$\approx \sum_{i=1}^{n} w_i g(t_i) \quad (3.9)$$

here t_i is the root of the nth order Legendre polynomial.

We can calculate the integration of the $2n - 1$ degree polynomial using n points with Gauss-Legendre numerical integration method.

Example 3.2.1 *Calculate the $\int_2^4 (x^2 - 1)dx$ integration analytically and using Gauss-Legendre numerical integration method.*

Table 3.1. n^{th} root of the Legendre polynomial

n	t_1	t_2	t_3	t_4	t_5	t_6	t_7	t_8	t_9	t_{10}
1	0	NA	NA	NA	NA	NA	NA	NA	NA	NA
2	−0.5773	0.5773	NA	NA	NA	NA	NA	NA	NA	NA
3	−0.7745	0.0000	0.7745	NA	NA	NA	NA	NA	NA	NA
4	−0.8611	−0.3399	0.3399	0.8611	NA	NA	NA	NA	NA	NA
5	−0.9061	−0.5384	0.0000	0.5384	0.9061	NA	NA	NA	NA	NA
6	−0.9324	−0.6612	−0.2386	0.2386	0.6612	0.9324	NA	NA	NA	NA
7	−0.9491	−0.7415	−0.4058	0.0000	0.4058	0.7415	0.9491	NA	NA	NA
8	−0.9602	−0.7966	−0.5255	−0.1834	0.1834	0.5255	0.7966	0.9602	NA	NA
9	−0.9681	−0.8360	−0.6133	−0.3242	0.0000	0.3242	0.6133	0.8360	0.9681	NA
10	−0.9739	−0.8650	−0.6794	−0.4333	−0.1488	0.1488	0.4333	0.6794	0.8650	0.9739

Table 3.2. n^{th} weight coefficient of Legendre polynomial

n	w_1	w_2	w_3	w_4	w_5	w_6	w_7	w_8	w_9	w_{10}
1	2	NA	NA	NA	NA	NA	NA	NA	NA	NA
2	1	1	NA	NA	NA	NA	NA	NA	NA	NA
3	0.555	0.0000	0.555	NA	NA	NA	NA	NA	NA	NA
4	0.34785	0.65214	0.65214	0.34785	NA	NA	NA	NA	NA	NA
5	0.2369	0.4786	0.5688	0.4786	0.2369	NA	NA	NA	NA	NA
6	0.1713	0.3607	0.4679	0.4679	0.3607	0.1713	NA	NA	NA	NA
7	0.1294	0.2797	0.3818	0.4179	0.3818	0.2797	0.1294	NA	NA	NA
8	0.1012	0.2223	0.3137	0.3626	0.3626	0.3137	0.2223	0.1012	NA	NA
9	0.0812	0.1806	0.2606	0.3123	0.3302	0.3123	0.2606	0.1806	0.0812	NA
10	0.0666	0.1419	0.2190	0.2692	0.2955	0.2955	0.2692	0.2190	0.1419	0.0666

We can calculate the integral analytically as:

$$\int_2^4 (x^2 - 1)dx = \frac{50}{3} \tag{3.10}$$

and Gauss-Legendre method $[2, 4] \to [-1, 1]$ then using the transformation $x = \frac{4-2}{2}t + \frac{4+2}{2} = t + 3$ we transform the integral

$$\int_2^4 (x^2 - 1)dx = \int_{-1}^1 [(t+3)^2 - 1]dt = \frac{50}{3}. \tag{3.11}$$

3.3. Two-Dimensional Numerical Integration

In the finite element method, when calculating the area integrals on the triangular element numerically, the Gaussian-quadrature method is generally used on the unit triangle domain. Gaussian points and corresponding weight coefficients required to apply this method are

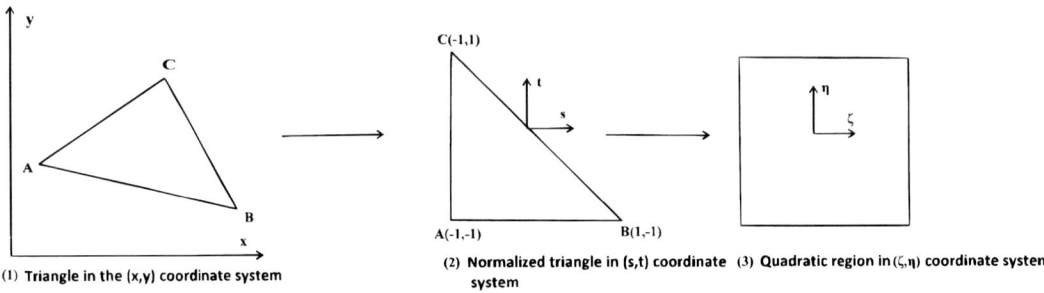

Figure 3.1. Numerical integral domain transformation

given in a finite number of tables in the literature. We will use an alternative numerical integral calculation method.

When calculating the integral over any triangular domain, the triangular domain 1 in Figure 6.7 is first transformed into the triangular region in 2, and then the triangular region in 1 is transformed into the quadratic region in 3.

Using this transformation, the roots of the Legendre polynomial of the desired degree are calculated on the quadratic region, and the numerical integral is calculated by using the desired number of points.

We can give the above domain transformations like below:

Let's transform the triangular region in 1 to the triangular region in 2 in Figure 6.7: Let the vertices of the triangular region in 1 be $A(x_1, y_1)$, $B(x_2, y_2)$, $C(x_3, y_3)$. Let's calculate the integral

$$I = \int_\Omega f(x, y) dx dy. \tag{3.12}$$

We first give the domain transformation;

$$\begin{aligned} x &= a_1 + b_1 s + c_1 t \\ y &= a_2 + b_2 s + c_2 t \end{aligned} \tag{3.13}$$

and we consider the shape functions as:

$$\begin{aligned} N_1 &= \frac{-1}{2}(s + t), \\ N_2 &= \frac{1}{2}(s + 1), \\ N_3 &= \frac{1}{2}(t + 1) \end{aligned}$$

Then using the equations in (3.13) and the corner points of the domain in Figure 6.7 1 and 2 we obtain

$$\begin{aligned} x_1 &= a_1 - b_1 - c_1 \\ y_1 &= a_2 - b_2 - c_2 \\ x_2 &= a_1 + b_1 - c_1 \end{aligned} \tag{3.14}$$

$$y_2 = a_2 + b_2 - c_2$$
$$x_3 = a_1 - b_1 + c_1$$
$$y_3 = a_2 - b_2 - c_2$$

we rewrite the equations in (3.14) with the matrix-vector form:

$$\begin{bmatrix} 1 & -1 & -1 \\ 1 & 1 & -1 \\ 1 & -1 & 1 \end{bmatrix} \begin{bmatrix} a_1 \\ b_1 \\ c_1 \end{bmatrix} = \begin{bmatrix} x_1 \\ x_2 \\ x_3 \end{bmatrix}$$

$$\begin{bmatrix} 1 & -1 & -1 \\ 1 & 1 & -1 \\ 1 & -1 & 1 \end{bmatrix} \begin{bmatrix} a_2 \\ b_2 \\ c_2 \end{bmatrix} = \begin{bmatrix} y_1 \\ y_2 \\ y_3 \end{bmatrix}$$

then $a_1, b_1, a_2, b_2, a_3, b_3$ are obtained with the form $x_1, y_1, x_2, y_2, x_3, y_3$ as follows.

$$\begin{aligned} a_1 &= \frac{x_2 + x_3}{2} \\ b_1 &= \frac{x_2 - x_1}{2} \\ c_1 &= \frac{x_3 - x_1}{2} \\ a_2 &= \frac{y_2 + y_3}{2} \\ b_2 &= \frac{y_2 - y_1}{2} \\ c_2 &= \frac{y_3 - y_1}{2}. \end{aligned} \qquad (3.15)$$

The determinant of the Jacobian matrix is

$$|J| = \begin{vmatrix} \frac{dx}{ds} & \frac{dx}{dt} \\ \frac{dy}{ds} & \frac{dy}{dt} \end{vmatrix} = \begin{vmatrix} \frac{x_2-x_1}{2} & \frac{x_3-x_1}{2} \\ \frac{y_2-y_1}{2} & \frac{y_3-y_1}{2} \end{vmatrix}$$

$$= \left(\frac{x_2 - x_1}{2}\right)\left(\frac{y_3 - y_1}{2}\right) - \left(\frac{x_3 - x_1}{2}\right)\left(\frac{y_2 - y_1}{2}\right)$$
$$= \frac{1}{4}(x_2 - x_1)(y_3 - y_1) - (x_3 - x_1)(y_2 - y_1) = \frac{AREA}{4}$$

then the integral (3.12) transforms to

$$I = \frac{AREA}{4} \int_{t=-1}^{1} \int_{s=-1}^{-t} f(x(s,t), y(s,t)) \, dt ds. \qquad (3.16)$$

we transform domain 1 in Figure 6.7 to domain 2.

Then we take

$$s = \zeta, \quad t = \frac{(1-\zeta)(1+\eta)}{2} - 1$$

and use in (3.15) to transform domain 1 to domain 2, and we obtain

$$\begin{aligned} x &= \frac{x_2 + x_3}{2} + \left(\frac{x_2 - x_1}{2}\right)\zeta + \left(\frac{x_3 - x_1}{2}\right)\left(\frac{(1-\zeta)(1+\eta)}{2} - 1\right) \\ y &= \frac{y_2 + y_3}{2} + \left(\frac{y_2 - y_1}{2}\right)\zeta + \left(\frac{y_3 - y_1}{2}\right)\left(\frac{(1-\zeta)(1+\eta)}{2} - 1\right) \end{aligned} \quad (3.17)$$

the Jacobian determinant for this domain transformation is

$$|J| = \begin{vmatrix} \frac{ds}{d\zeta} & \frac{ds}{d\eta} \\ \frac{dt}{d\zeta} & \frac{dt}{d\eta} \end{vmatrix} = \begin{vmatrix} 1 & 0 \\ \frac{-(1+\eta)}{2} & \frac{1-\zeta}{2} \end{vmatrix} = \frac{1-\zeta}{2}.$$

Using these transformations in integral (3.16),

$$I = \frac{AREA}{4} \int_{\zeta=-1}^{1} \int_{\eta=-1}^{1} f\left(x\left(\zeta, \frac{(1-\zeta)(1+\eta)}{2} - 1\right), \right. \\ \left. y\left(\zeta, \frac{(1-\zeta)(1+\eta)}{2} - 1\right)\right)\left(\frac{1-\eta}{2}\right)\right) dt ds \quad (3.18)$$

then integral I is calculated numerically as:

$$I = AREA \sum_{i=1}^{m} \sum_{j=1}^{n} \left(\frac{1-\zeta_i}{8}\right) w_i w_j f\left(\zeta_i, \frac{(1-\zeta_i)(1+\eta_j)}{2} - 1\right) \quad (3.19)$$

Chapter 4

Finite Element Method Solution of Laplace Equation

As the first example, using the boundary values of the function $\phi(x,y) = e^x \sin(y)$, which satisfies the Laplace equation on the unit circle in two-dimensional space, its solution is obtained by using the finite element method with Dirichlet-type boundary conditions. In Table 4.1, the numerical solution obtained using different element numbers and the $L2$ norm calculated using the real solution and the maximum error values are given. Although the results obtained with the coarse mesh (176 linear triangular elements) are convergent, it is observed that the L2 norm and the maximum error value decrease considerably when the number of elements is increased, as expected.

As the second example, using the function $\phi(r,\theta) = r^s(cos(s\theta) + sin(s\theta))$ which provides Laplace equation in polar coordinates on the unit circle, a numerical solution is obtained with Dirichlet-type boundary conditions and the L2 norm and maximum error values for the solutions obtained by using different numbers of elements for different s values ($s = 1$ and $s = 2$) are shown in Table 4.2. As the s value increases, it is observed from the $L2$ norm and maximum error values that the convergence in the numerical solution is also converging because the fluctuation period in the real solution increases.

Table 4.1. $L2$ norm for Laplace equation in the finite element method

Eleman Sayısı	L2 Norm	Maximum error
176	$0.000120 \to 10^{-4}$	$0.0039 \to 10^{-3}$
718	$0.0000169 \to 10^{-5}$	$0.0021 \to 10^{-3}$
2812	$0.00000200 \to 10^{-6}$	$0.000611 \to 10^{-4}$
11394	$0.000000252 \to 10^{-7}$	$0.000109 \to 10^{-4}$
45702	$0.0000000318 \to 10^{-8}$	$0.0000509 \to 10^{-5}$

In: Higgs Boson: A Mathematical Survey with Finite Element Method
Editors: Harun Selvitopi
ISBN: 979-8-88697-785-1
© 2023 Nova Science Publishers, Inc.

Table 4.2. $L2$ norm for Laplace equation using finite element method in polar coordinates for $s = 1$

Eleman Sayısı	$L2$ Norm	Maximum error
176	$0.00\ldots0137 \to 10^{-11}$	$0.00\ldots00507 \to 10^{-13}$
718	$0.00\ldots0584 \to 10^{-12}$	$0.00\ldots00982 \to 10^{-13}$
2812	$0.00\ldots0121 \to 10^{-12}$	$0.00\ldots0111 \to 10^{-12}$
11394	$0.00\ldots0199 \to 10^{-15}$	$0.00\ldots0328 \to 10^{-12}$
45702	$0.00\ldots0627 \to 10^{-14}$	$0.00\ldots0543 \to 10^{-12}$

Table 4.3. $L2$ norm for Laplace equation using finite element method in polar coordinates for $s = 2$

Eleman Sayısı	$L2$ Norm	Maximum error
176	$0.000288 \to 10^{-4}$	$0.00825 \to 10^{-3}$
718	$0.0000387 \to 10^{-5}$	$0.00277 \to 10^{-3}$
2812	$0.00000436 \to 10^{-6}$	$0.000758 \to 10^{-4}$
11394	$0.00\ldots0546 \to 10^{-7}$	$0.000191 \to 10^{-4}$
45702	$0.00\ldots0682 \to 10^{-8}$	$0.0000650 \to 10^{-5}$

Chapter 5

One-Dimensional Wave Equation

The wave equation is a hyperbolic type equation that includes a second derivative for time and space. One-dimensional wave equation has one space variable.

$$u_{tt}(x,t) = \Delta u = a^2 u_{xx}(x,t). \tag{5.1}$$

5.1. Finite Element Solution of One-Dimensional Wave Equation

In the Galerkin finite element method (GFEM) procedure, we produce the whole equation with the weight function satisfying the Kronecker delta property and then take integral over the solution domain,

$$\delta_{kl} = \begin{cases} 1, & k = l \\ 0, & k \neq l \end{cases}.$$

We apply the GFEM procedure considering w weight function,

$$u_{tt}(x,t)w = u_{xx}(x,t)w \tag{5.2}$$

then

$$\int_a^b (u_{tt}(x,t)w)dx = a^2 \int_a^b (u_{xx}(x,t)w)dx. \tag{5.3}$$

5.2. Central Difference Approximation

The time variable discretizes with the finite difference method. The central difference approximation will be used because the model includes a second derivative of the time variable,

$$\left(\frac{u^{n+1} - 2u^n + u^{n-1}}{k^2}, w\right) - \theta(\nabla u^{n+1}, \nabla w) - (1-\theta)(\nabla u^n, \nabla w), \tag{5.4}$$

In: Higgs Boson: A Mathematical Survey with Finite Element Method
Editors: Harun Selvitopi
ISBN: 979-8-88697-785-1
© 2023 Nova Science Publishers, Inc.

where $\theta = \frac{1}{2}$. Taking $\theta = \frac{1}{2}$, we have considered the Crank-Nicolson scheme due to the fact that it is second-order convergence.

Specifying a finite element discretization, the weak formulation becomes [4]

$$\left(\frac{u_h^{n+1} - 2u_h^n + u_h^{n-1}}{k^2}, w_h\right) - a^2\theta\left(\nabla u_h^{n+1}, \nabla w_h\right) - a^2(1-\theta)\left(\nabla u_h^n, \nabla w_h\right) = 0. \quad (5.5)$$

Then the weak formulation is got according to the time step as:

$$(u_h^{n+1}, w_h) - a^2 k^2 \theta (\nabla u_h^{n+1}, \nabla w_h) = 2(u_h^n, w_h) + a^2 k^2 (1-\theta)(\nabla u_h^n, \nabla w_h) - (u_h^{n-1}, w_h), \quad (5.6)$$

getting the systems of linear equations in the matrix form for the nth time step with the k step size as follows:

$$K[U^{n+1}] = H[U^n] - L[U^{n-1}], \quad (5.7)$$

where K, C, H and L are matrices with the entries

$$K_{ij} = \int_{x_i}^{x_{i+1}} \left(N_i N_j + \theta a^2 k^2 \frac{\partial N_i}{\partial x} \frac{\partial N_j}{\partial x}\right) dx$$

$$H_{ij} = \int_{x_i}^{x_{i+1}} \left(N_i N_j + (1-\theta) a^2 k^2 \frac{\partial N_i}{\partial x} \frac{\partial N_j}{\partial x}\right) dx$$

$$G_{ij} = \int_{x_i}^{x_{i+1}} (N_i N_j) dx,$$

then solving the matrix-vector system (5.7), we will obtain the GFEM solution of equation (5.1).

Example: Obtain the GFEM solution of the,

$$\frac{\partial^2 v(x,t)}{\partial t^2} - 4\frac{\partial^2 v(x,t)}{\partial x^2} = 0, \quad 0 < x < 1, \ 0 < t,$$

considering boundary conditions

$$v(0,t) = u(1,t) = 0, \quad \text{for} \ 0 < t,$$

and initial conditions

$$v(x,0) = sin(\pi x), \quad 0 \le x \le 1, \quad \text{and} \quad \frac{\partial^2 v(x,t)}{\partial t}(x,0) = 0, \quad 0 \le x \le 1.$$

Then compare the numerical results with the exact solution,

$$u(x,t) = sin(\pi x)cos(2\pi x).$$

Chapter 6

Finite Element Simulation of the One- and Two-Dimensional Wave Equation in Einstein and de Sitter Space-Time

The numerical solution of the wave equation in Einstein and de Sitter space-time using the Galerkin Finite element method (GFEM) with Crank-Nicolson scheme will be given in this chapter. For this purpose, we discretized the spatial variable with GFEM, and the temporal variable is discretized by the finite difference approximation. We acquired the numerical results with the Crank-Nicolson scheme.

The wave equation in Einstein and de Sitter space-time

$$\phi_{tt}(x,t) - t^{-4/3}\Delta\phi(x,t) + 2t^{-1}\phi_t(x,t) = f(x,t), \quad t > 0, \quad \vec{x} \in \mathbb{R}^n \tag{6.1}$$
$$\phi(x,0) = 0, \quad \phi_t(x,0) = 0.$$

has been introduced in 2010. The explicit depiction formulas and $L^p - L^q$ estimates for the solution were also given in the same year.

6.1. Application of the Numerical Method for One-Dimensional Problem

Taking $f(x,t) = 0$ and $n = 1$ the problem (6.1) transforms the

$$\phi_{tt}(x,t) - t^{-4/3}\Delta\phi(x,t) + 2t^{-1}\phi_t(x,t) = 0, \quad t > 0, \quad x \in \mathbb{R} \tag{6.2}$$
$$\phi(x,0) = 0, \quad \phi_t(x,0) = 0.$$

initial boundary value problem.

In the solution procedure we apply the finite difference approximation to discretize the temporal variable, and the Galerkin finite element method is also applied for the discretization of the spatial variable for problem (6.2).

In: Higgs Boson: A Mathematical Survey with Finite Element Method
Editors: Harun Selvitopi
ISBN: 979-8-88697-785-1
© 2023 Nova Science Publishers, Inc.

Applying the finite element method and using integration by parts for (6.2), we obtain the weak formulation of the equation given by employing linear function space $L = H_0^1(\Omega)$ as: $\phi \in L$ such that

$$(\phi_{tt}, w) + t^{-4/3}(\nabla \phi, \nabla w) + 2t^{-1}(\phi_t, w) = 0, \quad \forall w \in H_0^1(\Omega) \tag{6.3}$$

where $(.,.)$ represents the L_2 inner product.

Applying the central difference approximation to the time variable in (6.3), we obtain

$$\left(\frac{\phi^{k+1} - 2\phi^k + \phi^{k-1}}{\delta t^2}, w\right) + t^{-4/3}[\theta(\nabla \phi^{k+1}, \nabla w)$$
$$+ (1-\theta)(\nabla \phi^k, \nabla w)] + 2t^{-1}\left(\frac{\phi^{k+1} - \phi^k}{2\delta t}, w\right) = 0, \tag{6.4}$$

where $\theta = 1/2$. Then the variational formulation gets as:

$$(1 + t^{-1}\delta t)(\phi^{k+1}, w) + t^{-4/3}\delta t^2 \theta(\nabla \phi^{k+1}, \nabla w)$$
$$= -t^{-4/3}\delta t^2 (1-\theta)(\nabla \phi^k, \nabla w) - (1 - t^{-1}\delta t)(\phi^k, w) + 2(\phi^k, w) \tag{6.5}$$

The matrix form of the linear system of equations is obtained as follows:

$$H\left[\phi^{k+1}\right] = Q\left[\phi^k\right] + S\left[\phi^{k-1}\right] \tag{6.6}$$

where H, Q and S are matrices with the entries,

$$H_{ij} = \int_{x_i}^{x_{i+1}} \left[(1 + t^{-1}\delta t)N_i N_j + t^{-4/3}\delta t^2 \theta \frac{\partial N_i}{\partial x}\frac{\partial N_j}{\partial x}\right] dx$$

$$Q_{ij} = \int_{x_i}^{x_{i+1}} \left[(2 + t^{-1}\delta t)N_i N_j + t^{-4/3}\delta t^2 (1-\theta) \frac{\partial N_i}{\partial x}\frac{\partial N_j}{\partial x}\right] dx$$

$$S_{ij} = \int_{x_i}^{x_{i+1}} \left[-N_i N_j\right] dx$$

Applying central difference approximation to the initial condition $\phi_t(x, 0) = 0$, we obtain

$$\frac{\phi^{k+1} - \phi^{k-1}}{2\delta t} = 0. \tag{6.7}$$

If we use (6.7) in equation (6.6), we will obtain the system of linear equations with the matrix form as:

$$K\left[\phi^{k+1}\right] = Q[\phi^k] \tag{6.8}$$

where K is a matrix with the entire

$$K_{ij} = \int_{x_i}^{x_{i+1}} \left[(2 + t^{-1}\delta t)N_i N_j + t^{-4/3}\delta t^2 \theta \frac{\partial N_i}{\partial x}\frac{\partial N_j}{\partial x}\right] dx$$

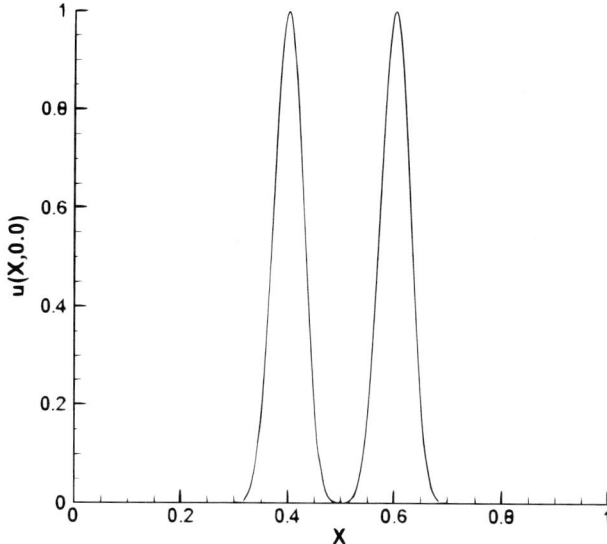

Figure 6.1. Bubble-like initial condition

During the solution process, the solution domain is taken to be $\Omega = [0, 1]$. The space and time step sizes are taken $\delta x = 10^{-2}$ and $\delta t = 10^{-2}$, respectively, and the initial function for the system (6.6) is taken,

$$B(x; C, R) = \begin{cases} exp\left(\frac{1}{R^2} - \frac{1}{R^2 - |x-C|^2}\right), & \text{if } |x - C| < R \\ 0, & \text{if } |x - C| > R \end{cases} \quad (6.9)$$

where $C \in \Omega$ is the center and R is the radius which satisfies $0 < R < 1$. $|x - C|$ denotes the Euclidean distance between x and C. And the boundary condition is taken $\phi(\partial\Omega, t) = 0$, where $\partial\Omega$ is the boundary of the solution domain (Ω). The initial condition is consider $\phi_0(x, 0) = 5 \times 10^{-2} B(x; 0.4, 0.2) + 5 \times 10^{-2} B(x; 0.6, 0.2)$ for the numerical solution of the system (6.6).

The acquired numerical results with the GFEM scheme are displayed by the graphics.

6.2. Application of the Numerical Method for Two-Dimensional Problem

Taking $f(x, t) = 0$ and $n = 2$ the problem (6.1) transforms the

$$\phi_{tt}(\vec{x}, t) - t^{-4/3}\Delta\phi(\vec{x}, t) + 2t^{-1}\phi_t(\vec{x}, t) = 0, \quad t > 0, \quad \vec{x} \in \mathbb{R}^2$$
$$\phi(\vec{x}, 0) = 0, \quad \phi_t(\vec{x}, 0) = 0. \quad (6.10)$$

initial boundary value problem.

In the solution procedure, we use a hybrid numerical method which consists of finite difference and finite element methods. The finite difference method has been used to discretize the temporal variable, and the finite element method has been used to discretize spatial

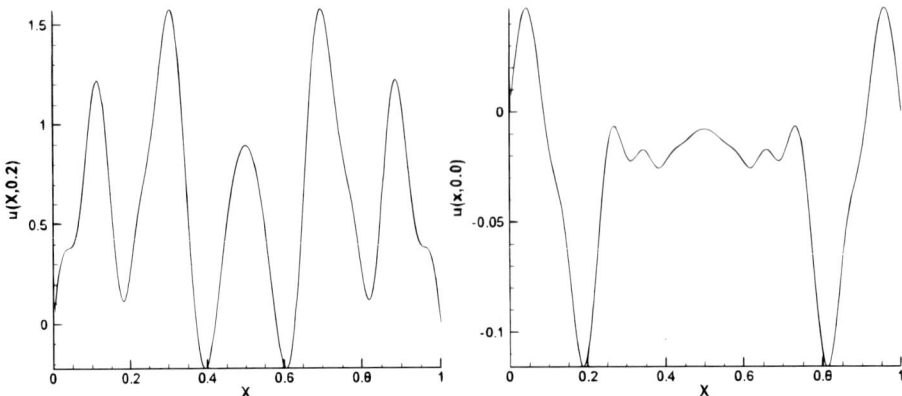

Figure 6.2. FEM solution of wave equation in Einstein and de Sitter space-time at 0.2(left), 0.6(right) time steps

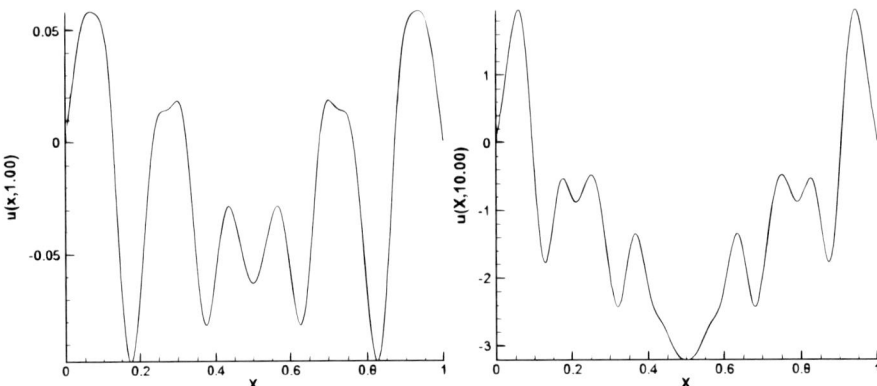

Figure 6.3. FEM solution of wave equation in Einstein and de Sitter space-time at 1(left), 10(right) time steps

variable. In the Galerkin finite element method first we multiply the full equation with the weight function and integrate it into the solution domain(Ω).

Applying the finite element method and using Green's second identity for (6.10), we obtain the weak formulation of the equation given by employing linear function space $L = H_0^1(\Omega)$ as: $\phi \in L$ such that

$$(\phi_{tt}, w) + t^{-4/3}(\nabla\phi, \nabla w) + 2t^{-1}(\phi_t, w) = 0, \quad \forall w \in H_0^1(\Omega) \tag{6.11}$$

where $(.,.)$ represents the L_2 inner product.

Applying the central difference approximation to the time variable in (6.11) we obtain

$$\left(\frac{\phi^{k+1} - 2\phi^k + \phi^{k-1}}{\delta t^2}, w\right) + t^{-4/3}[\theta(\nabla\phi^{k+1}, \nabla w)$$
$$+ (1-\theta)(\nabla\phi^k, \nabla w)] + 2t^{-1}\left(\frac{\phi^{k+1} - \phi^k}{2\delta t}, w\right) = 0, \tag{6.12}$$

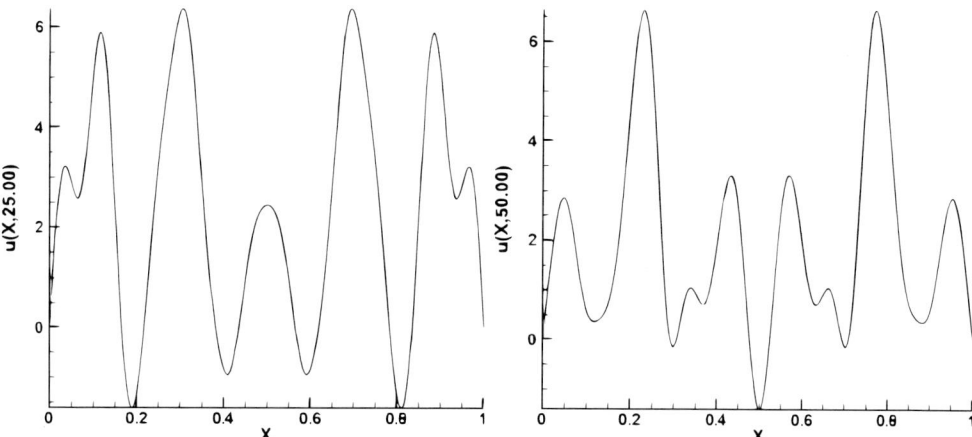

Figure 6.4. FEM solution of wave equation in Einstein and de Sitter space-time at 25(left), 50(right) time steps

where $\theta = 1/2$. Then the variational formulation gets as:

$$(1 + t^{-1}\delta t)(\phi^{k+1}, w) + t^{-4/3}\delta t^2 \theta (\nabla \phi^{k+1}, \nabla w)$$
$$= -t^{-4/3}\delta t^2 (1 - \theta)(\nabla \phi^k, \nabla w) - (1 - t^{-1}\delta t)(\phi^k, w) + 2(\phi^k, w) \quad (6.13)$$

The matrix form of the linear system of equations is obtained as follows:

$$H\left[\phi^{k+1}\right] = Q\left[\phi^k\right] + S\left[\phi^{k-1}\right] \quad (6.14)$$

where H, Q and S are matrices with the entries,

$$H_{ij} = \int_\Omega \left[(1 + t^{-1}\delta t)N_i N_j + t^{-4/3}\delta t^2 \theta \left(\frac{\partial N_i}{\partial x}\frac{\partial N_j}{\partial x} + \frac{\partial N_i}{\partial y}\frac{\partial N_j}{\partial y}\right)\right] d\Omega$$

$$Q_{ij} = \int_\Omega \left[(2 + t^{-1}\delta t)N_i N_j + t^{-4/3}\delta t^2 (1 - \theta) \left(\frac{\partial N_i}{\partial x}\frac{\partial N_j}{\partial x} + \frac{\partial N_i}{\partial y}\frac{\partial N_j}{\partial y}\right)\right] d\Omega$$

$$S_{ij} = \int_\Omega \left[-N_i N_j\right] d\Omega$$

Applying central difference approximation to the initial condition $\phi_t(x, 0) = 0$, we obtain

$$\frac{\phi^{k+1} - \phi^{k-1}}{2\delta t} = 0. \quad (6.15)$$

If we use (6.14) in equation (6.13), we will obtain the system of linear equations with the matrix form as:

$$K[\phi^{k+1}] = Q[\phi^k] \quad (6.16)$$

where K is a matrix with the entire

$$K_{ij} = \int_\Omega \left[(2 + t^{-1}\delta t)N_i N_j + t^{-4/3}\delta t^2 \theta \left(\frac{\partial N_i}{\partial x}\frac{\partial N_j}{\partial x} + \frac{\partial N_i}{\partial y}\frac{\partial N_j}{\partial y}\right)\right] d\Omega$$

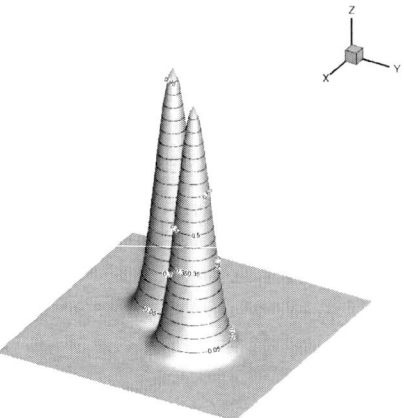

Figure 6.5. Bubble-like initial condition

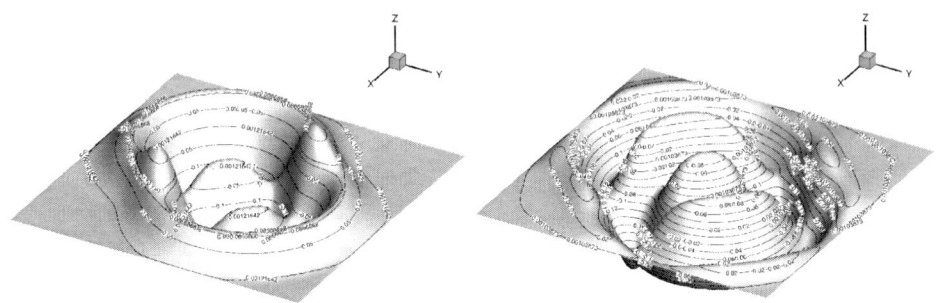

Figure 6.6. FEM solution of two-dimensional wave equation in Einstein and de Sitter space-time at 0.5(left), 1(right) time steps

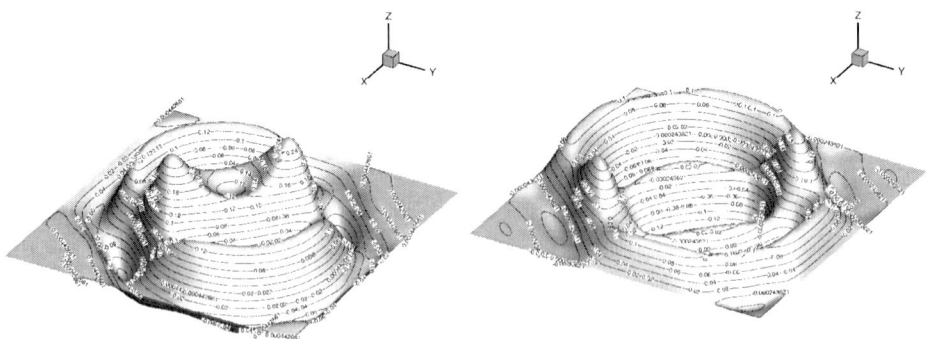

Figure 6.7. FEM solution of two-dimensional wave equation in Einstein and de Sitter space-time at 1.5(left), 2(right) time steps

During the solution process, the solution domain is taken to be $\Omega = [0, 1] \times [0, 1]$. The time step size is taken $\delta t = 10^{-2}$, and the initial function for the system (6.14) is taken:

$$B(x; x_0, R) = \begin{cases} \exp\left(\dfrac{1}{R^2} - \dfrac{1}{R^2 - \|x - x_0\|_2}\right), & \text{if} \quad \|x - x_0\|_2 < R \\ 0, & \text{if} \quad \|x - x_0\|_2 \geq R. \end{cases} \quad (6.17)$$

Chapter 7

Root Finding Approximations

In this chapter, we will scrutinize the root-finding methods which are well-known and most preferred numerical methods in detail.

7.1. Newton's Method

In the Newton's method procedure, our aim is to find the root of $f(x) = 0$. For this purpose, we use the Taylor expansion. Assume that $f \in C^2[a,b]$ and $x_0 \in [x_1, x_2]$ approximate to p, which satisfy $f'(x_0) \neq 0$ and $|x - x_0| < \epsilon$ where ϵ is very small, positive number. Let's consider the Taylor polynomial expanded about x_0,

$$f(x) = f(x_0) + (x - x_0)f'(x_0) + \frac{(x - x_0)^2}{2}f''(\eta(x)), \tag{7.1}$$

where $\eta(x)$ between x and x_0. Because of $f(x) = 0$, then equation be as:

$$f(x_0) + (x - x_0)f'(x_0) + \frac{(x - x_0)^2}{2}f''(\eta(x)) = 0. \tag{7.2}$$

The Newton method, is based on the $|x - x_0| < \epsilon$, then $|x - x_0|^2$ is much smaller, therefore

$$f(x_0) + (x - x_0)f'(x_0) \approx 0, \tag{7.3}$$

then the x obtained

$$x \approx x_0 - \frac{f(x_0)}{f'(x_0)} \equiv x_1, \tag{7.4}$$

then this iteration is repeated to

$$x_{n+1} = x_n - \frac{f(x_n)}{f'(x_n)}. \tag{7.5}$$

In: Higgs Boson: A Mathematical Survey with Finite Element Method
Editors: Harun Selvitopi
ISBN: 979-8-88697-785-1
© 2023 Nova Science Publishers, Inc.

We can write the Implicit Euler method as:

$$y_j = y_{j-1} + hf(x_j, y_j) \tag{7.6}$$

for the

$$\begin{cases} y' = f(x,y) \\ y(x_0) = y_0. \end{cases} \tag{7.7}$$

If we apply the Newton formulation to the given Implicit Euler method,

$$y_j^{n+1} = y_j^n - \frac{x_j(y_j)^2 - y_j^n + y_{j-1}\delta x}{2x_j(y_j)^n \delta x - 1}, \tag{7.8}$$

this iterative process continue up to $|y_j^{n+1} - y_j| < \epsilon$ or $x_j(y_j)^2 - y_j^n + y_{j-1}\delta x = 0$ is approximately satisfied, with initial guess y_{j-1}.

Example 7.1.1 *Find the root of $f(x) = cos(x) - x$ approximating with the Newton method.*

Solution 1. First we consider the derivative of $f'(x) = -sin(x) - 1$. Choosing the starting point $x_0 = \pi/4$, then applying Newton method

$$x_1 = x_0 - \frac{x_0}{f'(x_0)}$$

$$= \frac{\pi}{4} - \frac{cos(\frac{\pi}{4}) - \frac{\pi}{4}}{-sin(\frac{\pi}{4}) - 1}$$

$$= \frac{\pi}{4} - \frac{\sqrt{2}/2 - \frac{\pi}{4}}{-\sqrt{2}/2 - 1}$$

$$= 0.7395361337$$

$$p_2 = p_1 - \frac{cos(p_1) - p_1}{-sin(p_1) - 1}$$

$$= 0.7390851781$$

$$p_3 = p_2 - \frac{cos(p_2) - p_2}{-sin(p_2) - 1}$$

$$= 0.7390851332$$

$$p_4 = p_3 - \frac{cos(p_3) - p_3}{-sin(p_3) - 1}$$

$$= 0.7390851332$$

we can see the absolute difference between $|p_4 - p_3| < \epsilon = 10^{-12}$. The Newton method is a very powerful method to find the root of $f(x)$; however, we have to know the derivative of $f(x)$ in order to apply this method. We cannot know the derivative for every problem. Especially, in the numerical solution procedure for the nonlinear problems we cannot calculate the derivatives. To overcome this difficulty we can calculate it numerically.

7.1.1 Application of Newton Method

Therefore we have linearized the nonlinear system of equations using the Newton linearization method which is one of the most preferred linearization methods. For the linearization process, the first approximation of the solution of the nonlinear system given by $F(X) = 0$, be X_0. Then, to obtain the numerical solution takes into account the iterative method:

$$X_{k+1} = X_k - \mathcal{J}^{-1}(X_0)F(X_k), \quad \text{for} \quad k = 1, 2, \ldots \tag{7.9}$$

where $\mathcal{J}(X_0)$ is the Jacobian matrix of F in the vector X_0. The Jacobian matrix is calculated only in the first iteration of the iterative process.

It is impossible to find the Jacobian matrix analytically because the partial derivatives of $\mathcal{J}(X_0)$ are unknown. Therefore we will compute the Jacobian matrix approximately with the definition:

Definition 7.1.1 *(Jacobian matrix)*.

One Dimensional Case:
For $\Delta x > 0$, the approximation of the derivative as:

$$\frac{\partial F_i}{\partial X_j}(X_0) \approx \frac{F_i(X_0 + \overrightarrow{\Delta X}) - F_i(X_0)}{\Delta x} \quad \text{for} \quad i, j = 1, 2, \ldots, m \tag{7.10}$$

where $\overrightarrow{\Delta X} = \Delta x . e_j$ with being the jth canonical vector of $\mathbb{R}^n$.

With the approach (7.10) all the elements of the Jacobian matrix $\mathcal{J}(X_0)$ can be calculated. We know the $F(X_0)$, thereby using in the system (7.9) and solving the linear system, we obtain the X_1. This procedure will be repeated continuously up to satisfy the condition,

$$\|X_{k+1} - X_k\|_{L^\infty(\Omega)} < \epsilon, \quad \text{for any} \quad \epsilon > 0.$$

7.2. Secant Method

We can use the Secant method to accomplish finding the derivative of the function. The definition

$$f'(x_{n-1}) = \lim_{x \to x_{n-1}} \frac{f(x) - f(x_{n-1})}{x - x_{n-1}}$$

then x_{n-2} is very close to x_{n-1}, it becomes

$$f'(x_{n-1}) \approx \frac{f(x_{n-2}) - f(x_{n-1})}{x_{n-2} - x_{n-1}}$$

then consider the $f'(x_{n-1})$ last equation in the Newton's definition

$$x_n = x_{n-1} - \frac{f(x_{n-1})(x_{n-1} - x_{n-2})}{f(x_{n-1}) - f(x_{n-2})}$$

Exercise 1. Find the 3rd root of $f(x) = x^2 - 3$ starting $x_0 = 1$ with Newton and Secant methods.

Exercise 2. Find the 3rd root of $f(x) = -x^3 - cos(x)$ starting $x_0 = -1$ with Newton method.

Exercise 3. Find the 2nd root of $f(x) = x^2 + 3$ starting $x_0 = -1$ with,

- Newton Method
- Secant Method

Exercise 4. Find the 3rd root of $f(x) = sin(x) - x^2$ starting $x_0 = -1$ and $x_0 = 0$ with,

- Newton Method
- Secant Method

Exercise 5. Find the 3rd root of the below functions using the Newton method.

- $x^4 - 2x^2 + 5 = 0$, $[2, 5]$
- $x^3 - 2x^2 + 3x = 0$, $[-2, 2]$
- $sin(x) + 2x = 0$, $[0, \pi/2]$
- $cos(x) - x^2 = 0$, $[0, \pi/2]$

Exercise 6. Find the 3rd root of the below functions using the Newton method.

- $e^x - sin(x) = 0$, $[0, 3]$
- $cos(x) - 53^x + 9 = 0$, $[-3/2, 2]$
- $ln(x) + 5x^2 = 0$, $[0, 2]$
- $(x - 3)^3 + sin(2x) = 0$, $[2, 5]$
- $cos(x) + e^x = 0$, $[2, 5]$ and $[1, 3]$

Exercise 7. Find the 3rd root of the below functions using the Newton method.

- $e^x - sin(x) = 0$, $[0, 3]$
- $cos(x) - 53^x + 9 = 0$, $[-3/2, 2]$
- $ln(x) + 5x^2 = 0$, $[0, 2]$
- $(x - 3)^3 + sin(2x) = 0$, $[2, 5]$
- $cos(x) + e^x = 0$, $[2, 5]$ and $[1, 3]$

Exercise 8. Find the 5rd root of the below functions with the Newton and Secant methods.

- $2x^2 - e^2 = 0$, $[0, 2]$
- $2 - x + 2sin(x) = 0$, $[1, 2]$

Exercise 9. Find the 8rd root of the below functions with the Newton and Secant methods.

- $x^2 - 4x - 1 + e^x = 0$, $[0, 2]$
- $ln(x) + sin(x) - 4x = 0$, $[2, 4]$

Exercise 10. The $f(x) = 5x^4 + 9x^3 - 9x^2 + 11x - 8 = 0$ has two real zeros, in $[-3, -2]$ and $[0, 1]$. Find these roots approximating accuracy 10^{-7} using

- Newton Method
- Secant Method

Exercise 11. Solve the equation $x^3 - sin(2x) - cos(x) + e^x = 0$ using below methods considering 10^{-6} accuracy starting $x_0 = 2\pi$

- Newton Method
- Secant Method

Chapter 8

Newton's Method for Nonlinear System of Equations in $n-$Dimension

8.1. Newton Method

In one-dimensional case, we use the equality

$$k(x) = x - \psi(x)f(x)$$

to solve nonlinear problems. Here we choose $\psi = \frac{1}{f'(x)}$, where $f'(x) \neq 0$.

In $n-$dimension, we consider $\psi(x)$ function as a matrix as:

$$H(x) = \begin{bmatrix} h_{11}(x) & h_{12}(x) & \cdots & h_{1n}(x) \\ h_{21}(x) & h_{22}(x) & \cdots & h_{2n}(x) \\ \vdots & \vdots & & \vdots \\ h_{n1}(x) & h_{n2}(x) & \cdots & h_{nn}(x) \end{bmatrix} \quad (8.1)$$

the entries of H is a function $(h_{ij}(x))$ $\mathbb{R}^n \to \mathbb{R}$. Then to solve the system, we consider the equality

$$\mathbf{K}(\mathbf{x}) = \mathbf{x} - H(\mathbf{x})^{-1}\mathbf{F}(\mathbf{x}) \quad (8.2)$$

gives convergence to the solution of $\mathbf{F}(\mathbf{x}) = 0$, suppose $H(\mathbf{x})$ is a nonsingular matrix.

Theorem 1. *Let q be a solution of $K(x) = x$. Assume a number $\delta > 0$ which satisfies,*

1. *$\partial k_i / \partial x_j$ is continuous on $D_\delta = \{x | \|x-p\| < \delta\}$, for each $i = 1, 2, \ldots, n$ and $j = 1, 2, \ldots, n$.*
2. *$\partial_i^k(x)/(\partial x_j \partial x_k)$ is continuous, $|\partial_i^k(x)/(\partial x_j \partial x_k)| \leq N$, where $x \in D_\delta$ for each $i = 1, 2, \ldots, n$, $j = 1, 2, \ldots, n$ and $k = 1, 2, \ldots, n$.*
3. *$\partial k_i(p)/\partial x_j = 0$ for each $i = 1, 2, \ldots, n$ and $j = 1, 2, \ldots, n$.*

In: Higgs Boson: A Mathematical Survey with Finite Element Method
Editors: Harun Selvitopi
ISBN: 979-8-88697-785-1
© 2023 Nova Science Publishers, Inc.

Definition 8.1.1 *(Jacobian matrix).* The definition of the Jacobian matrix

$$J(x) = \begin{bmatrix} \frac{\partial f_1}{\partial x_1}(x) & \frac{\partial f_1}{\partial x_2}(x) & \cdots & \frac{\partial f_1}{\partial x_n}(x) \\ \frac{\partial f_2}{\partial x_1}(x) & \frac{\partial f_2}{\partial x_2}(x) & \cdots & \frac{\partial f_2}{\partial x_n}(x) \\ \vdots & \vdots & & \vdots \\ \frac{\partial f_n}{\partial x_1}(x) & \frac{\partial f_n}{\partial x_2}(x) & \cdots & \frac{\partial f_n}{\partial x_n}(x) \end{bmatrix}$$

Considering $H(x) = J(x)$ due to theorem (1), (8.2) becomes:

$$\mathbf{K}(\mathbf{x}) = \mathbf{x} - \mathbf{J}^{-1}(\mathbf{x})\mathbf{F}(\mathbf{x}) \tag{8.3}$$

then,

$$\mathbf{x}^{k+1} = \mathbf{K}(\mathbf{x}^k) = \mathbf{x}^k - \mathbf{J}^{-1}(\mathbf{x}^k)\mathbf{F}(\mathbf{x}^k) \tag{8.4}$$

this iteration is Newton's method for nonlinear systems.

Exercise 1. Solve the nonlinear system with the Newton method

$$3x - \cos(xy) - 1/2 = 0$$
$$x^2 - 81(y + 0.1)^2 + \sin(z) + 1.06 = 0$$
$$e^{xy} + 20z + \frac{10\pi - 3}{3} = 0$$

taking the starting point $x^0 = (1/10, 1/10, -1/10)^t$

Solution 1. Taking

$$\mathbf{F}(x, y, z) = (f(x, y, z), g(x, y, z), h(x, y, z))^t$$

considering

$$f(x, y, z) = 3x - \cos(xy) - 1/2$$
$$g(x, y, z) = x^2 - 81(y + 0.1)^2 + \sin(z) + 1.06$$
$$h(x, y, z) = e^{xy} + 20z + \frac{10\pi - 3}{3}$$

$$J(x, y, z) = \begin{bmatrix} 3 & z\sin(yz) & y\sin(yz) \\ 2x & -162(y + 0.1) & \cos(z) \\ -ye^{-xy} & -xe^{-xy} & 20 \end{bmatrix}$$

then $\mathbf{F}(\vec{x}^0) = (-0.199995, -2.269833417, 8.462025346)^t$ and the Jacobian matrix can be calculated

$$J(1/10, 1/10, -1/10) = \begin{bmatrix} 3 & 9.999833334 \times 10^{-4} & 9.999833334 \times 10^{-4} \\ 0.2 & -32.4 & 0.9950041653 \\ -0.09900498337 & -0.09900498337 & 20 \end{bmatrix}$$

then,

$$\vec{x}^1 = \vec{x}^0 - J^{-1}(\vec{x}_0)F(\vec{x}_0) = \begin{bmatrix} 0.4998696782 \\ 0.01946684853 \\ -0.5215204718 \end{bmatrix}$$

Table 8.1. The Newton method results with iterative process

k	x^k	y^k	z^k	$\|\vec{x}^{k+1} - \vec{x}^k\|_{\inf}$
1	0.1000000000	0.1000000000	−0.1000000000	
2	0.4998696728	0.194668485	−0.5125204718	0.4215204718
3	0.5000142403	0.0015885914	−0.5235569638	1.788×10^{-2}
4	0.5000000113	0.0000124448	−0.52359884500	1.576×10^{-3}
5	0.5000000000	8.516×10^{-10}	−0.5235987755	1.244×10^{-5}
6	0.5000000000	-1.375×10^{-11}	−0.5235987756	8.654×10^{-10}

go on the iteration for $k = 2, 3, \ldots$,

$$\begin{bmatrix} x^{k+1} \\ y^{k+1} \\ z^{k+1} \end{bmatrix} = \begin{bmatrix} x^k \\ y^k \\ z^k \end{bmatrix} + J^{-1}\left(\begin{bmatrix} x^k \\ y^k \\ z^k \end{bmatrix}\right) F\left(\begin{bmatrix} x^k \\ y^k \\ z^k \end{bmatrix}\right)$$

at the kth step Jacobian matrix and F function are

$$J(\vec{x}^{k+1}) = \begin{bmatrix} 3 & z^k \sin(y^k z^k) & y^k \sin(y^k z^k) \\ 2x^k & -162(y^k + 0.1) & \cos(z^k) \\ -y^k e^{-x^k y^k} & -x^k e^{-x^k y^k} & 20 \end{bmatrix}$$

and

$$F(\vec{x}^k) = \begin{bmatrix} 3x^k - \cos(x^k y^k) - 1/2 \\ (x^k)^2 - 81(y^k + 0.1)^2 + \sin(z^k) + 1.06 \\ e^{x^k y^k} + 20 z^k + \frac{10\pi - 3}{3} \end{bmatrix}.$$

Therefore the obtained results are shown in the table.

It is impossible to find the Jacobian matrix analytically for every problem as the partial derivatives of $J(x_0)$ are unknown. Therefore we will compute the Jacobian matrix approximately for the multivariate functions with the definition:

Definition 8.1.2 (*Jacobian matrix*). *For, $\delta x, \delta y > 0$ the approximation of derivative of the Jacobian matrix,*

$$\frac{\partial F_i}{\partial X_j}(X_0, Y_0) \approx \frac{F_i(X_0 + \vec{\delta X}, Y_0 + \vec{\delta y}) - F_i(X_0, Y_0)}{\delta x \delta y} \quad \text{for} \quad i, j = 1, 2, \ldots, m \quad (8.5)$$

where $\vec{\delta X} = \delta x e_j$ and $\vec{\delta Y} = \delta y e_j$ with e_j is being the jth canonical vector of $\mathbb{R}^n$.

Exercise 2. Find the third root of the below nonlinear systems using the Newton method with $\vec{x}^0 = \vec{0}$ starting point.

a)

$$4x^2 - 10x + 1/4y + 4 = 0,$$
$$1/2xy^2 + 2x - 5y + 4 = 0,$$

b)
$$\sin(4\pi xy) - y + 2x = 0,$$
$$e^x + 4ey^3 - 2e^2 x = 0,$$

c)
$$x(1 + 2x) + 2y = 6,$$
$$x^2 + 3y^2 = 15,$$

d)
$$5x^2 - y = 0,$$
$$y - 1/2(\sin(x) + \cos(y)) = 0,$$

Exercise 3. Find the third root of the below nonlinear systems using the Newton method with $\vec{x}^0 = \vec{0}$ starting point.

a)
$$x - \sin(yz) + 1 = 0,$$
$$1/2x^2 + 125y^2 + 3y - 2 = 0,$$
$$e^{-xy} + 10z + 5\pi = 0,$$

b)
$$5x - 3y^2 + y - 2z - 3 = 0,$$
$$4y + 2x^2 - 5 = 0,$$
$$4yz + 2 = 0,$$

c)
$$x^2 - 2y + 4 = 0,$$
$$x - y^2 - 3 = 0,$$
$$x + y + z - 5 = 0,$$

d)
$$5x + y^2 - 2z = 6,$$
$$x^2 + 5y - 2z = 7,$$
$$y^3 - 15z = -11,$$

Exercise 4. Find the third root of the below nonlinear systems using the Newton method within given interval.

a)
$$x + y^2 - 4z - 7 = 0,$$
$$x^2 + 10y - z - 5 = 0,$$
$$y^3 - 5z + 11 = 0,$$
$$0 \le x \le 1, 0 \le y \le 1, 0 \le z \le 1,$$
$$\text{and} \quad 0 \le x \le 1, 0 \le y \le 1, -1 \le z \le 1,$$

b)
$$3x - \cos(yz) - 1 = 0,$$
$$2x^2 + 25y^2 + 2y - 1 = 0,$$
$$e^{-2xy} + 10z - 3 = 0,$$
$$-1 \le x \le 1, -1 \le y \le 1, -1 \le z \le 1,$$

c)
$$x^2 + y - 19 = 0,$$
$$x - y^2 - 3 = 0,$$
$$x + y + z - 8 = 0,$$
$$-2 \le x \le 2, -2 \le y \le 2, -4 \le z \le 2,$$

d)
$$5x - 7y^2 - 3z - 4 = 0,$$
$$4y^2 + 2z^2 - 7 = 0,$$
$$4yz + 8 = 0,$$
$$0 \le x \le 1, 0 \le y \le 2, -2 \le z \le 2,$$

Exercise 5. Find the third root of the below nonlinear systems using the Newton method within given interval.

a)
$$2x^2 - 5y + 10 = 0,$$
$$xy^2 + 2x - 10y - 5 = 0,$$
$$0 \le x \le 1, 0 \le y \le 1,$$

b)
$$x(1-x) + 2y - 5 = 0,$$
$$(x-2)^2 + (3x-2)^2 = 0,$$
$$-1 \le x \le 1, -1 \le y \le 1,$$

c)
$$\cos(2\pi xy) - 2x - y = 0,$$
$$e^{-2x} + 2e + 2ex^2 - 2ex = 0,$$
$$-1 \le x \le 1, -2 \le y \le 1,$$

d)
$$2x^2 - y = 0,$$
$$x - 1/2xy = 0,$$
$$-2 \le x \le 2, -2 \le y \le 4,$$

Exercise 6. The below system has six solutions:

$$4x - y + z = zw,$$
$$-x + 3y - 2z = yz,$$
$$x - 2y + 3z = zw,$$
$$x^2 + y^2 + z^2 = 1,$$

- Prove if $(x, y, z, w)^t$ is a solution, then $(-x, -y, -z, w)^t$ is a solution.
- Find the third root of the system using the Newton method with 10^{-5} accuracy.

Exercise 7. Solve the nonlinear systems using the Newton method with 10^{-5} accuracy, using given starting points.

a)
$$3x^2 - 2y^2 = 0,$$
$$3xy^2 - x^3 - 2 = 0,$$
$$\vec{x}^0 = \begin{bmatrix} 1 \\ 2 \end{bmatrix}$$

b)
$$ln(x^2 + y^2) - cos(xy) - ln(3) + ln(2\pi) = 0,$$
$$e^{x-y} + sin(xy) = 0,$$
$$\vec{x}^0 = \begin{bmatrix} 1 \\ -1 \end{bmatrix}$$

c)
$$x^3 + x^2 y - xz - 5 = 0,$$
$$e^x + e^y - z = 0,$$
$$y^2 - 3xz - 4 = 0,$$
$$\vec{x}^0 = \begin{bmatrix} 1 \\ -1 \\ 2 \end{bmatrix}$$

d)
$$6x - 2cos(yz) - 5 = 0,$$
$$7x + x^2 + cos(z) - 3 = 05e^{-xy} + 10z + 2\pi = 0,$$
$$\vec{x}^0 = \begin{bmatrix} 0 \\ 0 \\ 0 \end{bmatrix}$$

Exercise 8. The Jacobian matrix of the nonlinear system is singular. Considering $\vec{x}^0 = (1, 1, -2)^t$ as starting point, apply the Newton method.

Hint : The convergence shouldn't be plausible or gingerly.

$$3x - \cos(yz) - 0.5 = 0,$$
$$x^2 - 125y^2 - 1 = 0,$$
$$e^{-xy} + 10z + 5\pi - 3 = 0,$$

8.2. Quasi-Newton Method

In the Newton method, we calculate the Jacobian matrix and take the inverse of this matrix at each step. But this causes more computational cost. To accomplish this we can use the Quasi-Newton method which has the algorithm:

$Given \ \vec{x}^0$
$Set \ B_0 = I$
$If \ x_l \ is \ solution \ (\nabla f(x_l) \approx 0) \ Exit$
$Solve \ B_l P_l = -\nabla f(x_l)$
$\alpha_l^1 = 1$
$While \ f(x_l + \alpha_l^n P_l) > f(x_l) + a_1 \alpha_l^n P_l^T \nabla f(x_l)$
$\alpha_l^{n+1} = \dfrac{\alpha_l^n}{2}$
$x_{l+1} = x_l + \alpha_l P_l = x_l + \alpha_l P_l$
$S_l = x_{l+1} - x_l$
$y_l = \nabla f(x_{l+1}) - \nabla f(x_l)$
$B_{l+1} = B_l + \dfrac{(y_l - B_l S_l)(y_l - B_l S_l)^T}{(y_l - B_l S_l)^T S_l}$

8.3. Broyden Method

Find the approximation solution of a given system of nonlinear equations $F(\vec{x}) = \vec{0}$ with the starting point $\vec{x}^0$.

Consider starting approximation $\vec{x} = (x_1, x_2, \ldots, x_n)^T$ and tolerance number ϵ using N max number of iteration. The Broyden method has the algorithm:

$Set \ J(\vec{x})_{i,j} = \dfrac{\partial f_i}{\partial x_j}(\vec{x});$
$\vec{u} = F(\vec{x}) \ (\vec{u} = F(\vec{x}^0))$
$J = J^{-1}(\vec{x})$
$\vec{h} = -J\vec{u} \ (\vec{h} = \vec{h}_1)$
$\vec{x} = \vec{x} + \vec{h}$
$l = 2$
$While \ (l \leq N)$

$$\vec{v} = \vec{u}$$
$$\vec{u} = F(\vec{x}) \quad (\vec{u} = F(\vec{x}^l))$$
$$\vec{w} = \vec{u} - \vec{v} \quad (\vec{w} = \vec{w}_l)$$
$$\text{Set} \quad \vec{y} = -J\vec{w} \quad (\vec{y} = -J_l^{-1}\vec{w}_l)$$
$$\text{Set} \quad q = -\vec{h}^T \vec{y}$$
$$\text{Set} \quad \vec{z}^T = \vec{h}^T J$$
$$\text{Set} \quad J = J + \frac{1}{q}(\vec{h} + \vec{y})\vec{z}^T \quad (J = J_{l+1^{-1}})$$
$$\text{Set} \quad \vec{h} = -J\vec{u} \quad (\vec{h} = -J_l^{-1} F(\vec{x}^l))$$
$$\text{Set} \quad \vec{x} = \vec{x} + \vec{h}$$
$$\text{If} \quad \|\vec{h}\| < \epsilon \quad OUTPUT(\vec{x})$$
$$\text{Set} \quad l = l+1$$
$$OUTPUT$$
$$STOP$$

Exercise 9. Solve the nonlinear systems using the Broyden method with 10^{-3} accuracy, using given starting points.

a)
$$2x^2 - 10x + 4 = 0,$$
$$xy^2 + 3x - 7y + 3 = 0,$$
$$\vec{x}^0 = \begin{bmatrix} 0 \\ 1 \end{bmatrix}$$

b)
$$2x^2 - 3y^2 = 0,$$
$$2xy^2 - x^3 - 5 = 0,$$
$$\vec{x}^0 = \begin{bmatrix} 1 \\ -1 \end{bmatrix}$$

c)
$$\cos(xy) - 2x + \pi y = 0,$$
$$e^{-x} + 2y^2 - 3x = 0,$$
$$\vec{x}^0 = \begin{bmatrix} 0 \\ -1 \end{bmatrix}$$

d)
$$e^{-xy} - \sin(\pi xy) = 0,$$
$$\ln(x^2 + 2y^2) - \cos(xy) = 0$$
$$\vec{x}^0 = \begin{bmatrix} 2 \\ 0 \end{bmatrix}$$

Exercise 10. Solve the nonlinear systems using the Broyden method with 10^{-3} accuracy, using given starting points.

a)
$$2x - \ln(z^2 + 3y^2) - 2 = 0,$$
$$2x - 125y - 2y + 5 = 0,$$
$$y^2 - 3yz - 4 = 0,$$
$$\vec{x}^0 = \begin{bmatrix} 0 \\ 0 \\ 0 \end{bmatrix}$$

b)
$$4x - 3\cos(yz) - 2 = 0,$$
$$x - y^2 + 2z + 1 = 0,$$
$$x + y + z - 4 = 0,$$
$$\vec{x}^0 = \begin{bmatrix} 1 \\ -1 \\ 0 \end{bmatrix}$$

c)
$$x^2 + y - 8 = 0,$$
$$x - y + 3 = 0,$$
$$x + y - 3yz - 4 = 0,$$
$$\vec{x}^0 = \begin{bmatrix} 0 \\ 0 \\ 0 \end{bmatrix}$$

d)
$$x^2 + y^3 - 5z = 0,$$
$$x - 2y^2 - 3z + 5 = 0,$$
$$x^2 - y^2 z + 2 = 0,$$
$$\vec{x}^0 = \begin{bmatrix} -1 \\ 2 \\ 2 \end{bmatrix}$$

Exercise 11. Solve the nonlinear systems using the Broyden method with 10^{-5} accuracy, using given starting points.

a)
$$3x^2 - 2y^2 = 0,$$
$$3xy^2 - x^3 - 2 = 0,$$
$$\vec{x}^0 = \begin{bmatrix} 1 \\ 2 \end{bmatrix}$$

b)
$$\ln(x^2+y^2) - \cos(xy) - \ln(3) + \ln(2\pi) = 0,$$
$$e^{x-y} + \sin(xy) = 0,$$
$$\vec{x}^0 = \begin{bmatrix} 1 \\ -1 \end{bmatrix}$$

c)
$$x^3 + x^2y - xz - 5 = 0,$$
$$e^x + e^y - z = 0,$$
$$y^2 - 3xz - 4 = 0,$$
$$\vec{x}^0 = \begin{bmatrix} 1 \\ -1 \\ 2 \end{bmatrix}$$

d)
$$6x - 2\cos(yz) - 5 = 0,$$
$$7x + x^2 + \cos(z) - 3 = 05e^{-xy} + 10z + 2\pi = 0,$$
$$\vec{x}^0 = \begin{bmatrix} 0 \\ 0 \\ 0 \end{bmatrix}$$

Exercise 12. The below system has six solutions:
$$4x - y + z = zw,$$
$$-x + 3y - 2z = yz,$$
$$x - 2y + 3z = zw,$$
$$x^2 + y^2 + z^2 = 1,$$

- Prove if $(x, y, z, w)^t$ is a solution, then $(-x, -y, -z, w)^t$ is a solution.
- Find the third root of the system using the Broyden method with 10^{-5} accuracy.

Exercise 13. The Jacobian matrix of the nonlinear system is singular. Considering $\vec{x}^0 = (1, 1, -2)^t$ as starting point, apply the Broyden method.

Hint : The convergence shouldn't be plausible or gingerly.
$$3x - \cos(yz) - 0.5 = 0,$$
$$x^2 - 125y^2 - 1 = 0,$$
$$e^{-xy} + 10z + 5\pi - 3 = 0,$$

Chapter 9

Finite Difference/Galerkin Finite Element Simulation of the Semi-Linear Wave Equation with Scale-Invariant Damping, Mass and Power Nonlinearity

The focus of this study is on numerical simulation of the semi-linear wave equation with damping term, mass and power nonlinearity.

$$\begin{aligned}\phi_{tt} - \Delta\phi + \frac{\mu}{1+t}\phi_t + \frac{v^2}{(1+t)^2}\phi &= |\phi|^p, \quad x \in \mathbb{R}^n, \quad t > 0 \\ \phi(x,0) &= \phi_0(x), \quad x \in \mathbb{R}^n, \\ \phi_t(x,0) &= \phi_1(x), \quad x \in \mathbb{R}^n,\end{aligned} \quad (9.1)$$

where $p > 1$ and $\mu > 0$ and v are real constants.

It is difficult to obtain the exact solution to the nonlinear variable coefficient "wave-like" problems. Therefore we acquire the numerical solutions of the aforementioned $1+1$ IBVP. As a solution procedure the spatial variable and the temporal variable of the equation in (9.1) are discretized using the GFEM and FDM, respectively. To the accuracy of the numerical solution the FDM-FDM scheme in which spatial and temporal variables are discretized using the FDM is also applied to the equation in (9.1).

The quantity which describes the relationship between the damping term $\frac{\mu}{1+t}u_t$ and the mass term $\frac{v^2}{(1+t)^2}u$ is $\delta = (\mu-1)^2 - 4v^2$ [??]. In this study, the relation between μ and v is considered $\delta = 1$.

Through the transformation $\phi(x,t) = (1+t)^{\frac{-\mu}{2}}u(x,t)$ in (9.1) we obtain the following initial boundary value problem:

$$\begin{aligned}u_{tt} - \Delta u &= (1+t)^{\frac{-\mu}{2}(p-1)}|u|^p, \quad (x,t) \in [0,1] \times [0,\infty), \\ u(x,0) &= u_0(x) \\ u_t(x,0) &= u_1(x)\end{aligned} \quad (9.2)$$

where $\mu > 0$.

In: Higgs Boson: A Mathematical Survey with Finite Element Method
Editors: Harun Selvitopi
ISBN: 979-8-88697-785-1
© 2023 Nova Science Publishers, Inc.

9.1. Application of the GFEM

Applying the Galerkin finite element method for (9.2) [4], we obtain the weak formulation of the equation given by employing linear function space $L = H_0^1(\Omega)$ as: $u \in L$ such that

$$(u_{tt}, w) + (\nabla u, \nabla w) - (1+t)^{\frac{-\mu}{2}(p-1)}(|u|^p, w) = 0, \qquad w \in H_0^1(\Omega) \tag{9.3}$$

where $(.,.)$ represents the L^2- inner product.

Using the central difference discretization for the temporal variable in (9.3) we obtain

$$\left(\frac{u^{n+1} - 2u^n + u^{n-1}}{\Delta t^2}, w\right) = -[\theta(\nabla u^{n+1}, \nabla w) + (1-\theta)(\nabla u^{n-1}, \nabla w)] \\ + (1+t)^{\frac{-\mu}{2}(p-1)}(|u^n|^p, w), \tag{9.4}$$

where $\theta \in \{1/2, 1\}$.

Specifying a finite element discretization, the weak formulation becomes [4]: Find $u_h \in L_h$ such that

$$\left(\frac{u_h^{n+1} - 2u_h^n + u_h^{n-1}}{\Delta t^2}, w_h\right) = -[\theta(\nabla u_h^{n+1}, \nabla w_h) + (1-\theta)(\nabla u_h^{n-1}, \nabla w_h)] \\ + (1+t)^{\frac{-\mu}{2}(p-1)}(|u_h^n|^p, w_h), \qquad \forall w_h \in L_h \tag{9.5}$$

Then the weak formulation is obtained according to the time step as:

$$\left(u_h^{n+1}, w_h\right) + \Delta t^2 \theta(\nabla u_h^{n+1}, \nabla w_h) = (2u_h^n, w_h) - \Delta t^2(1-\theta)(\nabla u_h^{n-1}, \nabla w_h) \\ - (u_h^{n-1}, w_h) + (1+t)^{\frac{-\mu}{2}(p-1)}\Delta t^2(|u_h^n|^p, w_h). \tag{9.6} \\ \text{for} \quad n = 0, 1, \ldots, N \quad \text{and} \quad \forall w_h \in L_h$$

We will get the systems of nonlinear equations in the matrix form for the nth time step with the Δt step size as follows:

$$K[u^{n+1}] - C[u^n] + H[u^{n-1}] - G[|u^n|^p] = 0. \tag{9.7}$$

where K, C, H and G are matrices with the entries

$$K_{ij} = \int_{x_i}^{x_{i+1}} \left(N_i N_j + \theta \Delta t^2 \frac{\partial N_i}{\partial x} \frac{\partial N_j}{\partial x}\right) dx$$

$$C_{ij} = \int_{x_i}^{x_{i+1}} 2N_i N_j dx$$

$$H_{ij} = \int_{x_i}^{x_{i+1}} \left(N_i N_j + (1-\theta)\Delta t^2 \frac{\partial N_i}{\partial x} \frac{\partial N_j}{\partial x}\right) dx$$

$$G_{ij} = \int_{x_i}^{x_{i+1}} \left(\Delta t^2 (1+t)^{\frac{-\mu}{2}(p-1)} |N_i|^p N_j\right) dx$$

The initial condition

$$u_t(x, 0) = 0 \tag{9.8}$$

is discretized with the central difference approximation for the initial time step as:

$$\frac{u^{n+1} - u^n}{2\Delta t} = 0. \tag{9.9}$$

Applying (9.9) to the system (9.7) the system of nonlinear equations for the initial time step is obtained as follows:

$$S[u^{n+1}] - C[u^n] - G[|u^n|^p] = 0. \tag{9.10}$$

where S is a matrix with the entry

$$S_{ij} = \int_{x_i}^{x_{i+1}} \left(2N_i N_j + \Delta t^2 \frac{\partial N_i}{\partial x} \frac{\partial N_j}{\partial x} \right) dx$$

9.2. Application of the FDM

The FDM is used for the accuracy of the numerical results obtained by the GFEM for equation in (9.1).

We employ the central difference approximation to the spatial and temporal variables for equation in (9.1). We denote $x_l = l\Delta x$, for $l = 0, 1, \ldots, s$ with the space step length $\Delta x = \frac{1}{s}$ and $t_m = m\Delta t$, for $m = 0, 1, \ldots, h$ with the time step length $\Delta t = \frac{1}{h}$.
We propose the following FDM scheme for equation in (9.1):

$$\begin{aligned}
&\frac{u_i^{n+1} - 2u_i^n + u_i^{n-1}}{\Delta t^2} - \theta \left(\frac{u_{i+1}^{n+1} - 2u_i^{n+1} + u_{i-1}^{n+1}}{\Delta x^2} \right) \\
&- (1-\theta) \left(\frac{u_{i+1}^{n-1} - 2u_i^{n-1} + u_{i-1}^{n-1}}{\Delta x^2} \right) - (1+t)^{\frac{-\mu}{2}(p-1)} |u_i^n|^p = 0
\end{aligned} \tag{9.11}$$

where $u_i^n = u(x_i, t_n)$, and $\theta \in \{1/2, 1\}$. If we denote the mesh ratio $c = \frac{\Delta t^2}{\Delta x^2}$, then (9.11) is rewritten with respect to time step as:

$$\begin{aligned}
&-c\theta u_{i+1}^{n+1} + (1 + 2c\theta)u_i^{n+1} - c\theta u_{i-1}^{n+1} - c(1-\theta)u_{i+1}^{n-1} + (1 + 2c(1-\theta))u_i^{n-1} \\
&- c(1-\theta)u_{i-1}^{n-1} - c(1-\theta)u_{i-1}^{n-1} - 2u_i^n - (1+t)^{\frac{-\mu}{2}(p-1)} \Delta t^2 |u_i^n|^p = 0.
\end{aligned} \tag{9.12}$$

If we set $\vec{U}^n = [u_1^n, u_2^n, \ldots, u_m^n]^T$, we rewrite (9.5) with matrix form

$$(I + c\theta A)\vec{U}^{n+1} + (I + c(1-\theta)A)\vec{U}^{n-1} - 2\vec{U}^n - (1+t)^{\frac{-\mu}{2}(p-1)}|\vec{U}^n|^p = 0. \tag{9.13}$$

where I is the unit of the matrix and

$$A = \begin{bmatrix} 2 & -1 & 0 & \cdots & & 0 \\ -1 & 2 & -1 & 0 & & 0 \\ 0 & \ddots & \ddots & \ddots & & \vdots \\ 0 & & \ddots & -1 & 2 & -1 \\ 0 & & \cdots & 0 & -1 & 2 \end{bmatrix}.$$

9.3. Application of Newton Method

We use the Newton Method to (9.7) which is one of the fastest linearization methods to linearize the system of nonlinear equations.

Let X_0 be the first approximation of the solution of the nonlinear system given by $F(X) = 0$. Then, to acquire the numerical solution take account of the iterative method:

$$X_{k+1} = X_k - J^{-1}(X_0)F(X_k), \quad \text{for} \quad k = 1, 2, \ldots \tag{9.14}$$

where $J(X_0)$ is the Jacobian matrix of F in the vector X_0. The Jacobian matrix is calculated only in the first iteration of the iterative process.

The iterative system of (9.7) is rewritten for each $(n+1)^{th}$ time step as follows:

$$KX + a = 0.$$

where $a = -C[u^n] + H[u^{n-1}] - G[|u^n|^p]$ and $X = u^{n+1}$. Denoting

$$F(X) = KX - C[u^n] + H[u^{n-1}] - G[|u^n|^p], \tag{9.15}$$

then to acquire the approximate solution of system (9.15), the Newton method is applied to calculate the root of $F(X)$.

Due to the partial derivative ($\frac{\partial F_i}{\partial X_j}$), where i is the (i^{th}) row vector of F according to variable X_j, of the $F(X)$ are not known. Therefore the approximate derivative will be used to compute Jacobian matrix $J(X_0)$.

For $\Delta x > 0$, the approximation of the derivative is

$$\frac{\partial F_i}{\partial X_j}(X_0) \approx \frac{F_i(X_0 + \overrightarrow{\Delta X}) - F_i(X_0)}{\Delta x} \quad \text{for} \quad i,j = 1, 2, \ldots, m \tag{9.16}$$

where $\overrightarrow{\Delta X} = \Delta x . e_j$ with being the jth canonical vector of $\mathbb{R}^n$.

With the approach (9.16) all the elements of the Jacobian matrix $J(X_0)$ can be calculated. We know $F(X_0)$, thereby using in system (9.14) and solving the linear system, we obtain the X_1. This procedure will be repeated continuously to satisfy the condition,

$$\|X_{k+1} - X_k\|_{L^\infty(\Omega)} < \epsilon, \quad \text{for any} \quad \epsilon > 0.$$

Chapter 10

Higgs Boson in de Sitter Space-Time

10.1. Mathematical Model of the Higgs Boson in de Sitter Space-Time

The mathematical model of a lot of physical events is to be introduced by the hyperbolic partial differential equations. Since the hyperbolic equations describe how waves propagate, they are also called wave-type equations. One such equation, the Higgs boson equation, has an important role in quantum physics, the theory of relativity, particle physics, general relativity, astrophysics and cosmology. The de Sitter metric describes the exponential expansion of the universe. In order to examine the motion of matter in more detail, the Higgs boson equation in the expanding universe has been obtained. The Higgs boson equation in de Sitter space-time is modeled by applying the de Sitter metric obtained by applying the Lemaître-Robertson transform to the line element belonging to this space, to the equation of motion in the scalar field. It is estimated that the Higgs boson is the particle that gives matter its mass. The movement of matter will be observed with the solution obtained by considering the mass of matter in this equation obtained in de Sitter space-time. The Higgs boson equation is semi-linear in structure and is a partial differential equation with a time dimension of 1 and a space dimension of 2. Many studies have been carried out on the Higgs boson equation since 1926, when it was introduced in Minkowski space, but most of the studies were carried out by considering the one-dimensional space variable.

As is known, the Higgs boson, which is thought to be in the standard model of particle physics, was first observed for a very short time in an experiment at CERN in 2012. With the numerical solution of the current mathematical model, the simulation of the Higgs boson according to the time level will be obtained. This simulation is intended to provide more detailed information about the behavior of the Higgs boson over time. Moreover, with the simulation to be obtained, it will provide horizons for experimental physicists working on the observation of the Higgs Decay. In addition, the obtained numerical solution will guide in obtaining the analytical (real) solution to the aforementioned problem.

As a result, the transfer of the Higgs boson equation to Sitter space-time is an important development for better observation of the motion of matter. It is clear that numerically

---

In: Higgs Boson: A Mathematical Survey with Finite Element Method
Editors: Harun Selvitopi
ISBN: 979-8-88697-785-1
© 2023 Nova Science Publishers, Inc.

solving this mathematical model and obtaining the simulation will give important information about the motion of the Higgs boson in the standard model of particle physics.

The mathematical model of the Higgs boson equation in de Sitter space-time is as:

$$\begin{aligned} v_{tt} + H\phi_t - e^{-2Ht}\Delta v + m^2\phi = |\psi|^{p-1} v, & \quad (x,t) \in \Omega \times [0,T], \\ v(x,0) = \varphi_0(x) & \quad x \in \Omega, \\ v_t(x,0) = \varphi_1(x) & \quad x \in \Omega, \\ v(x,t) = 0, & \quad (x,t) \in \partial\Omega \times [0,T]. \end{aligned} \quad (10.1)$$

Here, H represents the Hubble constant, m is physical mass and $p > 1$. Moreover, system (10.1) has the total energy which is given by expression

$$E(t) = e^{Ht}\left[\frac{1}{2}\left\|\frac{\partial v}{\partial t} + \frac{H}{2}v\right\|_{x,2}^2 + \frac{e^{-2t}}{2}e^{-2t}\|\nabla v\|_{x,2}^2 - \frac{1}{2}\left(\frac{H^2}{4} + 1\right)\|\psi\|_{x,2}^2 \right. \\ \left. + \frac{1}{q+1}\|v\|_{x,q+1}^{q+1}\right], \quad \forall t \in [0,T] \quad (10.2)$$

Actually, it is easy to see that

$$E' = -e^{Ht}\left[e^{-2t}\|\nabla v\|_{x,2}^2 + \frac{q-1}{1(q+1)}\|v\|_{x,q+1}^{q+1}\right], \quad \forall t \in [0,T]. \quad (10.3)$$

The exact solution of system (10.1) has not been obtained yet. Therefore we focus on the numerical solution of this problem. For this purpose, we have considered the hybrid numerical method which consists of finite difference and finite element methods. For the discretization of the temporal variable we use the finite difference method, and we use the finite element method for the discretization of the spatial variable. For simplicity we use the transformation $v = e^{-nHt}\psi$, equation in (10.1); the Higgs boson equation in de Sitter space-time has the following form:

$$\begin{aligned} \psi_{tt} - e^{-2t}\Delta\psi + M^2\psi = |e^{\frac{-nH}{2}t}\psi|^{p-1}\psi & \quad (x,t) \in \Omega \times [0,T], \\ \psi(x,0) = \psi_2(x), & \quad x \in \Omega, \\ \psi_t(x,0) = \psi_3(x), & \quad x \in \Omega, \\ \psi(x,t) = 0, & \quad (x,t) \in \partial\Omega \times [0,T], \end{aligned} \quad (10.4)$$

where $M^2 = m^2 - \frac{n^2 H^2}{4}$.

10.2. Finite Element Method for Higgs Boson Equation

In this section, we discuss the standard Galerkin FEM solution for the Higgs boson equation in de Sitter space-time in detail. Our numerical approach for problem (10.4) with the u_2 boundary condition is to apply FEM for the spatial discretization and FDM for the temporal discretization. For the linearization of the obtained nonlinear system of equations using FEM for the equation in (10.4), we consider the Newton method. We also calculate the Jacobian matrix numerically in the linearization process.

We apply the FEM to equation in (10.4) in the rectangular solution domain $\Omega_1 = [-1, 1] \times [-1, 1]$ in two spatial dimensions with the boundary conditions $\psi(\partial\Omega_1, t) = 0$ and $\psi(\partial\Omega_2, t) = 0$, respectively, where $t > 0$. Then by using the linear function space $L = (H_0^1(\Omega))$, we obtain the weak formulation to find $\psi \in L$ for the nonlinear form

$$B(\psi_{tt}, w) + e^{-2t} B(\nabla\psi, \nabla w) + M^2 B(\psi, w) = e^{\frac{-nH}{2}t} B(\psi^p, w), \quad \forall w \in L, \qquad (10.5)$$

where $B(\psi, w)$ denotes the bilinear form, $B(\psi, w) = \int_\Omega (\psi.w) d\Omega$.

With the triangulation of the solution domain considering finite dimensional subspaces $L_h \in L$, the variational formulation is written. Then, the weak formulation becomes for the linear form [4]: Find $\psi_h \in L_h$

$$B(\psi_{h_{tt}}, w_h) + e^{-2t} B(\nabla\psi_h, \nabla w_h) + M^2 B(\psi_h, w_h) = e^{\frac{-nH}{2}t} B(\psi_h^p, w_h), \quad \forall w_h \in L. \qquad (10.6)$$

For the discretization of the temporal variable, we use the central difference approximation (CDA), and we also use the FEM to discretize the spatial variable for (??) and (10.6), then the weak formulation becomes:

$$\left(\frac{\psi^{k+1} - 2\psi^k + \psi^{k-1}}{\tau^2}, w\right) = -[e^{-2t_{k+1}}\theta(\nabla\psi^{k+1}, \nabla w) + e^{-2t_k}(1-\theta)(\nabla\psi^k, \nabla w)]$$
$$- M^2[\theta(\psi^{k+1}, w) + (1-\theta)(\psi^k, w)]$$
$$+ (e^{\frac{-nH}{2}t_{k+1}\theta}(\psi^{k+1})^p, w)$$
$$+ (e^{\frac{-nH}{2}t_k(1-\theta)}(\psi^k)^p, w), \qquad (10.7)$$

where δt denotes the time step size.

Then, we obtain the matrix form of the system of nonlinear equations as:

$$\delta t^2 \left(\left(\frac{1}{\delta t^2} + \theta M^2 \delta t^2\right) C + \theta K\right) [\Psi^{k+1}] + \theta \delta t^2 e^{\frac{-nH}{2}t_{k+1}} G[(\Psi^{k+1})^p]$$
$$+ \delta t^2 \left(\frac{-2}{\delta t^2} + (1-\theta)M^2\right) C + (1-\theta)K\right) [\Psi^k] \qquad (10.8)$$
$$- (1-\theta)\delta t^2 e^{\frac{-nH}{2}t_k} G[(\Psi^k)^p] - C[\Psi^{k-1}] = 0,$$

where
$K = \int_\Omega \left(e^{-2t_{k+1}} \delta t^2 \left(\frac{\partial N_i}{\partial x}\frac{\partial N_j}{\partial x} + \frac{\partial N_i}{\partial y}\frac{\partial N_j}{\partial y}\right)\right) d\Omega$,
$G = \int_\Omega \tau^2 N_i^p N_j d\Omega$,
$C = \int_\Omega N_i N_j d\Omega$.

For the initial time step ($k = 0$) equation (10.8) becomes the following form:

$$\delta t^2 \left(\left(\frac{1}{\delta t^2} + \theta M^2 \delta t^2\right) C + \theta K\right) [\Psi^1] + \theta \delta t^2 e^{\frac{-nH}{2}t_1} G[(\Psi^1)^p]$$
$$+ \delta t^2 \left(\frac{-2}{\delta t^2} + (1-\theta)M^2\right) C + (1-\theta)K\right) [\Psi^0] \qquad (10.9)$$
$$- (1-\theta)\delta t^2 e^{\frac{-nH}{2}t_0} G[(\Psi^0)^p] - C[U^{-1}] = 0,$$

respectively. We apply the central difference approximation for the initial condition $u_t(x, 0) = u_3$ to approximate u^{-1} as:

$$\frac{\psi^1(x) - \psi^{-1}(x)}{2\delta t} = \psi_3(x), \quad x \in \Omega_2. \tag{10.10}$$

Equation (10.9) with equation (10.10) becomes the following matrix form:

$$\delta t^2 \left(\left(\frac{2}{\delta t^2} + \theta M^2 \delta t^2 \right) C + \theta K \right) [\Psi^1] + \theta \delta t^2 e^{\frac{-nH}{2} t_1} G[(\Psi^1)^p] +$$
$$\delta t^2 \left(\frac{-2}{\delta t^2} + (1 - \theta) M^2 \right) C + (1 - \theta) K \right) [\Psi^0] \tag{10.11}$$
$$- (1 - \theta) \delta t^2 e^{\frac{-nH}{2} t_0} G[(\Psi^0)^p] - 2\delta t \psi_3 C = 0.$$

10.2.1 Newton Method

In this subsection, we will apply the Newton linearization method which is one of the fastest linearization methods to linearize the nonlinear system of equations in (10.8).

X_0 is the first approximation of the nonlinear system of equations $F(X) = 0$. Then, we will consider the iterative procedure:

$$X_{l+1} = X_l - \mathcal{J}^{-1}(X_0) F(X_l), \quad \text{for} \quad l = 1, 2, 3, \ldots \tag{10.12}$$

to acquire the approximate solution of the nonlinear system (10.8). Here, $\mathcal{J}(X_0)$ is the Jacobian matrix of the F in the vector X_0.

The iteration (10.12) will be repeated when the $\|X_{l+1} - X_l\|_2 < \epsilon$ condition is satisfied. The nonlinear system can be arranged according to $(k+1)^{th}$ time step as:

$$KX + \xi = 0,$$

where
$\xi = \tau^2 \left(\frac{-2}{\tau^2} + (1 - \theta) M^2 \right) C + (1 - \theta) K \right) [\Psi^k] - (1 - \theta) \delta t^2 e^{\frac{-nH}{2} t_k} G[(\Psi^k)^p] - C[\Psi^{k-1}]$ and $X = \Psi^{k+1}$. Representing

$$F(X) = KX - \delta t^2 \left(\frac{-2}{\delta t^2} + (1 - \theta) M^2 \right) C + (1 - \theta) K \right) [\Psi^k]$$
$$- (1 - \theta) \delta t^2 e^{\frac{-nH}{2} t_k} G[(\Psi^k)^p] - C[\Psi^{k-1}], \tag{10.13}$$

then the Newton method is applied to find the root of $F(X)$ to acquire the solution of system (10.13).

In the iterative process, we consider the convergence condition $\epsilon = 10^{-8}$, and during the calculation process, the convergence condition is satisfied.

The determination of the Jacobian matrix is an important part of the Newton method. Due to the unknown of the partial derivatives of the $F(X)$, it is impossible to find the Jacobian matrix analytically. Therefore we will calculate the Jacobian matrix approximately as in the definition below.

Definition 10.2.1 *(Jacobian matrix). For, $\delta x, \delta y > 0$ the approximation of derivative of the Jacobian matrix,*

$$\frac{\partial F_i}{\partial X_j}(X_0, Y_0) \approx \frac{F_i(X_0 + \vec{\delta X}, Y_0 + \vec{\delta y}) - F_i(X_0, Y_0)}{\delta x \delta y} \quad \text{for} \quad i, j = 1, 2, \ldots, m \quad (10.14)$$

where $\vec{\delta X} = \delta x e_j$ and $\vec{\delta Y} = \delta y e_j$ with e_j is the jth canonical vector of $\mathbb{R}^n$.

10.3. Numerical Results

In this section, we present the numerical tests for equation (10.4) by changing the values of the mass $m > 0$ for the different initial conditions.

We also consider the numerical solution of $u(x, y, t)$ for (10.4) problem in the rectangular space domain $\Omega_2 = [-1, 1] \times [-1, 1]$ with $t \geq 0$. Fortran software is used for numerical tests.

For the numerical solutions, the time step is taken as $\delta t = 0,001$.

In the solution procedure, the domain of the problems has discretized 5408 linear triangular elements obtained from 2809 discretization points, and we have considered the compact support initial function as:

$$B(x; x_0, R), = \begin{cases} \exp\left(\frac{1}{R^2} - \frac{1}{R^2 - \|x - x_0\|_2}\right), & \text{if} \quad \|x - x_0\|_2 < R \\ 0, & \text{if} \quad \|x - x_0\|_2 \geq R. \end{cases} \quad (10.15)$$

$x_0 \in \mathbb{R}^2$ and R is the radius satisfying $R > 0$ for the initial conditions (see, e.g., [8]). In addition, we take the zero boundary conditions for the numerical examples of (10.8).

Example 10.3.1 *We have considered the standard sine-Gordon equation as:*

$$\psi_{tt} + \psi_t - \Delta \psi + \sin(\psi) = 0, \quad (x, y) \in \Omega_3, \quad t > 0, \quad (10.16)$$

which have been obtained from the Higgs boson equation under some special circumstances. The analytical solution of equation (10.16) is [??]

$$\psi(x, y, t) = 4 \arctan(\exp(x + y - t)). \quad (10.17)$$

We have put forth that the system possesses an energy conservation law

$$E(t) = E(0), \quad (10.18)$$

where the energy is

$$E(t) = \frac{1}{2} \int_{\Omega_3} [\psi_t^2 + \psi_x^2 + \psi_y^2 + 2(1 - \cos\psi)] dx dy, \quad (10.19)$$

and the computational domain has been taken $\Omega_3 = [-10, 10] \times [-3, 3]$ for the energy. In Figure 10.1, one can observe from the numerical results that the energy is exactly preserved,

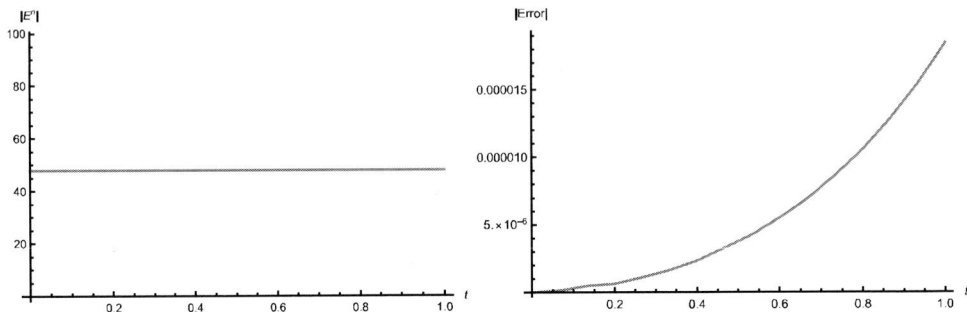

Figure 10.1. The total energy(left) and the error in energy(right) for Example 3.1.

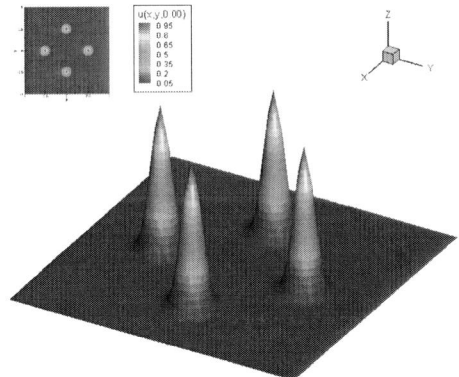

Figure 10.2. Bubble-like initial condition for $m = \sqrt{6}$ and p=3

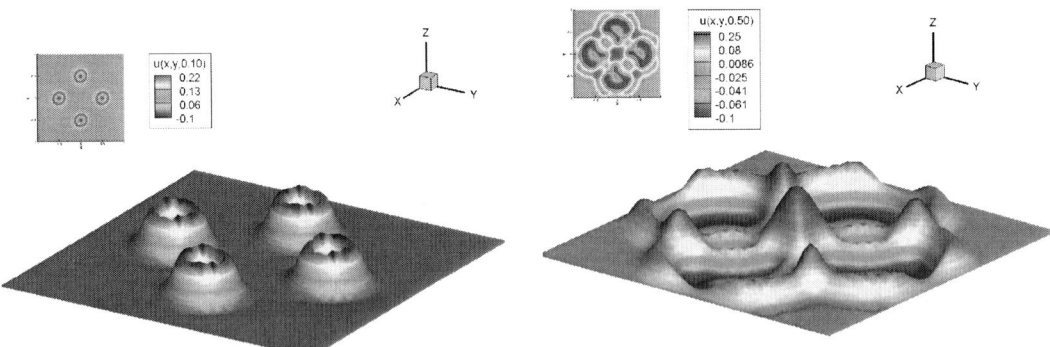

Figure 10.3. FEM solution of Higgs boson equation in de Sitter space-time at 0.1(left), 0.5(right) time steps for m=6 and p=3

which is compatible with [11]. One can also see on the right side of Figure 10.1 that the total energy error ($|E(t) - E(0)|$) of our scheme is very close to zero. We can say the energy is conserved at any time level due to the total energy error being very close to zero.

Example 10.3.2 *Define x_1, x_2, x_3 and $x_4 \in \mathbb{R}^2$ as: $x_1 = (0.5, 0)$, $x_2 = (-0.5, 0)$, $x_3 = (0, -0.5)$ and $x_4 = (0, 0.5)$.*

Higgs Boson in de Sitter Space-Time

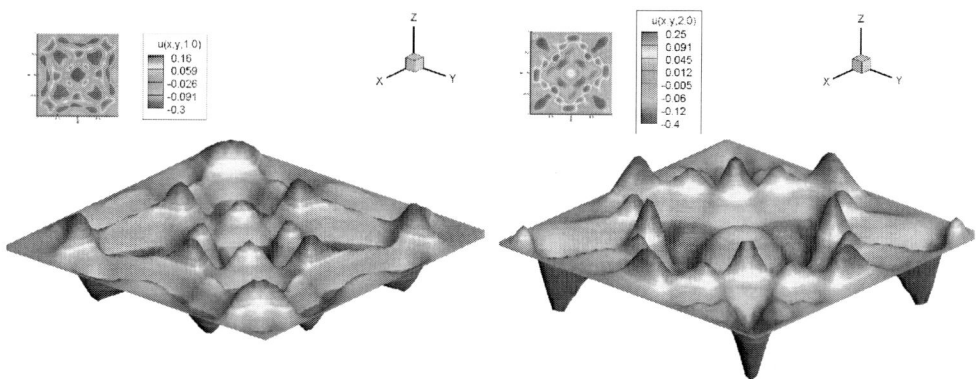

Figure 10.4. FEM solution of Higgs boson equation in de Sitter space-time at 1(left), 2(right) time steps for m=6 and p=3

$$B(x; x_0, R) = \begin{cases} u_2(x) = B(x, x_1, 0.3) + B(x, x_2, 0.3) \\ \qquad\quad + B(x, x_3, 0.3) + B(x, x_4, 0.3), \quad \forall \vec{x} \in \Omega_2, \\ u_3(x) = -5u_2(x), \quad \forall \vec{x} \in \Omega_2. \end{cases} \qquad (10.20)$$

Figure 10.2 shows the initial condition (10.16).

References

[1] H. Selvitopi (2022), Numerical Solution of the One and Two Dimensional Semi-Linear Wave Equation with Scale-Invariant Damping, Mass and Power Non-Linearity with θ-Scheme, Advances in Mathematics Research, Nova Science Publishers, 30, 221–237.

[2] Davies, A. J. (2011) The Finite Element Method: An Introduction with Partial Differential Equations, Second Edition, Oxford University Press Inc., New York.

[3] Logon, D. L. (2010) A First Course In The Finite Element Method, Fifth Edition, Cengage Learning, USA.

[4] Reddy JN. (1993) An introduction to the finite element method, New York: McGraw-Hill.

[5] Burden, R.L., Faires D.J., Burden, A.M. (2016) Numerical Analysis, Tenth Edition, Cengage Learning, USA.

[6] Yagdjian K (2012) On the global solution of the Higgs boson equation. Comm Part Diff Equa 37(3):447–478.

[7] Yagdjian K, Balogh A (2018) The maximum principle and sign changing solutions of the hyperbolic equation with the Higgs potential. J Math Anal Appl 465: 403–422.

[8] Balogh A, Banda J, Yagdjian K (2019) High-Performance Implementation of a Runge-Kutta Finite-Difference Scheme for the Higgs Boson Equation in the de Sitter Spacetime. Commun Nonlinear Sci 68: 15–30.

[9] Selvitopi H, Yazici M (2019) Numerical Results For The Klein-Gordon Equation in de Sitter Spacetime. Mathematical Methods in the Applied Sciences 42: 5446–5454.

[10] Tsuchiya T, Nakamura M (2019) On the Numerical Experiments of the Cauchy Problem for Semi-Linear Klein-Gordon Equation in the de Sitter Spacetime. J Comput Appl Math 361: 378–412.

[11] Zaky MA, Handy AS (2020) An efficient dissipation–preserving Legendre–Galerkin spectral method for the Higgs boson equation in the de Sitter spacetime universe. Applied Numerical Mathematics 160: 281–295.

[12] Muñoz-Pérez LF, Macías-Díaz JE, Guerrero JA (2020) A dissipation-preserving finite-difference scheme for a generalized Higgs boson equation in the de Sitter space–time. Appl Math Lett 107: 106425.

[13] Muñoz-Pérez LF, Macías-Díaz JE (2020) On the solution of a generalized Higgs boson equation in the de Sitter space-time through an efficient and Hamiltonian scheme. Journal of Computational Physics 417: 109568.

[14] Macías-Díaz JE (2020) Design and analysis of a dissipative scheme to solve a generalized multi-dimensional Higgs boson equation in the de Sitter space–time. Journal of Computational and Applied Mathematics 113120.

[15] H. Selvitopi, M. Zaky, A. S. Hendy, (2021), Crank-Nicolson/finite element approximation for the Schrödinger equation in the de Sitter spacetime, Physica Scripta, 96, 124010.

[16] H. Selvitopi (2022), Stabilized Fem solution of magnetohydrodynamic flow in different geometries, Journal of Scientific Reports-A, 049, 105–117.

[17] H. Selvitopi (2022), Numerical investigation of damped wave type MHD flow with time-varied external magnetic field, Chinese Journal of Physics, 80, 127–147.

[18] D. Irk, E. Kirli, M. Zorsahin Görgülü (2022), A High order accurate numerical solution of the Klein-Gordon equation, Appl. Math. Inf. Sci. 16(2), 331-339.

[19] J.M. Ortega (1988), Introduction to parallel and vector solution of linear systems, Plenum Press, New York, 305.

[20] J.M. Ortega (1972), Numerical Analysis; a second course, Academic Press, New York, 201.
[21] J.M. Ortega, Jr. W. G. Poole, (1981), An introduction to numerical methods for differential equations, Pitman Publishing, Marshfield, MA.
[22] G. D. Smith, (1965), Numerical solution of partial differential equations, Oxford University Press Inc., New York.
[23] O. C. Zienkiewicz, K. Morgan (1983), Finite elements and approximation, John Wiley and Sons, New York.
[24] H. Farzana S. M. Karim (2012) Accurate Evaluation Schemes for Triangular Domain Integrals, IOSR Journal of Mechanical and Civil Engineering, 2(6).
[25] H. Selvitopi (2022), Finite difference/Finite element simulation of the two-dimensional linear and nonlinear Higgs boson equation in the de Sitter space-time, Engineering with Computers, 30, 891–900.

Index

A

Application of the numerical method
   for one-dimensional problem, 47–49
   for two-dimensional problem, 49–52

B

Backward-difference method, 7–9
Broyden method, 65–68

C

Computational molecule of 1D heat equation
   with Crank-Nicolson finite difference method, 10
   with explicit finite difference method, 6
   with implicit finite difference method, 8
Computational molecule of 1D wave equation
   with Crank-Nicolson finite difference method, 22
   with explicit finite difference method, 20, 21
   with implicit finite difference method, 21
Crank-Nicolson method, 9–11
   matrix-vector form, 14–15
Crank-Nicolson scheme, 47

D

de Sitter space-time, 73
   bubble-like initial condition, 78
   FEM solution of Higgs boson equation, 78, 79
   finite element method, 74–76
      Newton method, 76–77
   mathematical model, 73–74
   numerical results, 77–79
   one- and two-dimensional wave equation, 47–52
   total energy and error in energy, 78
Dirichlet-type boundary conditions, 43
Discretization, 29
   of 1D heat equation, 6
   error, 3
   points and elements, 30, 31
   of the solution domain, 4
Domain discretization, 2

E

Einstein and de Sitter space-time
   FEM solution of two-dimensional wave equation, 52
   FEM solution of wave equation, 50, 51
Elements, 27, 29–30
Elliptic equations, finite difference method (FDM), 1–5

F

Finite difference approximation
   solution of wave equation, 24–25
Finite difference/Galerkin finite element simulation, 69
   application of Newton Method, 72
   application of the FDM, 71
   application of the GFEM, 70–71
Finite difference method (FDM), 71
   computational molecule of 1D heat equation
      with Crank-Nicolson, 10
      with explicit, 6
      with implicit, 8
   computational molecule of 1D wave equation
      with Crank-Nicolson, 22
      with explicit, 20, 21
      with implicit, 21
   discretization of 1D heat equation, 6
   discretization of the solution domain, 4
   domain discretization, 2
   elliptic equations, 1–5
   grid points and numerical solutions at time, 23
   hyperbolic partial differential equations, 18–23
      stability analysis, 23–25
   parabolic equations, 5
      backward-difference method, 7–9
      Crank-Nicolson method, 9–11
      exercises, 15–17
      forward-difference method, 5–7
      stability analysis, 11–15
Finite element method (FEM); *see also individual entries*
   application of, 29
      2-D elements, 30–31
      discretization, 29
      elements, 29–30
      formulation for Laplace equation, 32
      shape functions, 31

triangular elements shape functions, 31–32
variational form for Laplace
equation, 34–35
weak form for Laplace equation, 32–34
development of, 27–28
discretization points and elements, 30
$L2$ norm for Laplace equation, 43
polar coordinates for $s = 1$, 44
polar coordinates for $s = 2$, 44
numbering order of discretization points, 30
solution of Laplace equation, 43–44
Finite element simulation, Einstein and de sitter space-time
application of the numerical method
for one-dimensional problem, 47–49
for two-dimensional problem, 49–52
bubble-like initial condition, 49, 52
FEM solution of two-dimensional wave equation, 52
FEM solution of wave equation, 50, 51
Forward difference approximation
results and exact solution of the heat equation, 7, 9, 12
Forward-difference method, 5–7
Fourier stability method (Von Neumann stability analysis), 11–13
Function spaces, 32

G

Galerkin finite element method (GFEM), 45–47, 70–71
Gauss-type integration methods, 38
Gauss-Legendre method, 38–39
Grid points and numerical solutions, 23

H

Higgs boson equation, 73; *see also individual entries*
bubble-like initial condition, 78
FEM solution of, 78, 79
finite element method, 74–76
Newton method, 76–77
mathematical model, 73–74
numerical results, 77–79
total energy and error in energy, 78
Hyperbolic partial differential equations, FDM, 18–23
stability analysis, 23–25

J

Jacobian matrix, 55, 76–77

L

Laplace equation

finite element method form, 32
variational form, 34–35
weak form, 32–34
Legendre polynomial
n^{th} root of the, 39
n^{th} weight coefficient, 39

M

Matrix method, 14–15
Matrix-vector system, 8

N

Newton method, 53–54, 59–65, 72
application of, 55
integration
Simpson method, 38
Trapezium rule, 37
Nonlinear system of equations in n-dimension, 59
Broyden method, 65–68
Newton method, 59–65
Quasi-Newton method, 65
Numbering order of discretization points, 30
Numerical integral domain transformation, 40
Numerical integration methods, 37
Gauss-type integration methods, 38
Gauss-Legendre method, 38–39
newton-type integration methods
Simpson method, 38
Trapezium rule, 37
two-dimensional numerical integration, 39–42

O

One-dimensional problem, 47–49
One-dimensional wave equation, 45
central difference approximation, 45–46
finite element solution of, 45

P

Parabolic equations, finite difference method (FDM), 5
backward-difference method, 7–9
Crank-Nicolson method, 9–11
exercises, 15–17
forward-difference method, 5–7
stability analysis, 11–15
Partial differential equations (PDE), *see* Finite difference method (FDM); Finite element method (FEM)

Q

Quasi-Newton method, 65

R

Root finding approximations, 53
    Newton's method, 53–54
        application of, 55
    Secant method, 55–57
Round-off error, 3

S

Secant method, 55–57
Semi-linear wave equation, *see* Finite difference/Galerkin finite element simulation
Shape functions, 31
Simpson method, 38
Stability analysis
    Fourier stability method (Von Neumann stability analysis), 11–13
    matrix method, 14–15
Structural analysis, 28

T

Taylor expansion, 53
Trapezium rule, 37
Triangle and quadrilateral-type elements, 30–31
Triangular elements shape functions, 31–32
Truncation error, 3
Two-dimensional numerical integration, 39–42
Two-dimensional problem, 49–52
2-D elements, 30–31